D0616371

Meditation within Eternity

*Becoming One with the
Consciousness of the Universe*

By Eric Pepin

Higher Balance Publishing
Portland, Oregon

*This book has been transcribed and compiled
from live lectures given by Eric Pepin.
Some elements of the live format have been preserved.*

Published by Higher Balance Institute
515 NW Saltzman Road #726, Portland, Oregon 97229
www.higherbalance.com

ISBN: 978-0-9759080-6-8

Library of Congress Control Number: 2012931826

Meditation within Eternity / Eric Pepin

Published 2012.
Printed in the United States of America.

Dedicated to Eric Robison.

To whom made so many things possible and taught me the meaning of friend. The one I never chose.

To the fellowship, Matthew Robison, Jamison Priebe, and Thomas Rutledge, on the long and winding road.

The Navigators who, with great determination, sewed straw into gold-leaf to be shared with all: Vivien Fedd, Amy Provost, Loretta Huinker, John A, Sean M, Jenny G, Adam V, Brady Heberle, Dianne B, Irina I, Joe Salvador, Matt Krebs, Mai-Liis Sepp, Molly McDermott, Nicholas Ciervo, and Ray Ross.

To all those who believe they are not seen, felt or heard...
I see you and I have always believed in you.

To God... forever & ever.

TABLE OF CONTENTS

Introduction

MORE THAN TWENTY-FIVE years have passed during my pursuit of higher consciousness and sixth sense awareness; always asking real questions regarding reality and existence. Little did I realize when I first began this quest, that one day my personal experiences would help others. Yet, here it is.

This book is a faithful reflection of this journey. It is an important resource to provide astonishing tools, developed along the way that revolutionized my journey into the unknown. I am so excited to share the wonders that await you.

My advice for your journey is while you grow a garden of life within you, be patient. Do not limit yourself to expectations or personal desires; allow the Universe to perfect you on Its terms. Do not reflect on failures, but rather, on your successes.

Experiencing ups and downs is part of the master plan the universe has for you. Feeling empowered empowers you. Have patience, your true nature and dimensional consciousness will unveil itself to you.

Meditation within Eternity is more than it first appears. Over time it will reveal more to you no matter how often read. Knowledge, in truth, is a dimensional key. It is a perfect resignation of your frequency that unlocks hidden doors within your dimensional mind.

Each time it is used, it opens a new place. Be sure to review the material occasionally, no matter how well you know it. Share it with others. Collectively, your minds will become another key to open new levels.

You are about to embark on the greatest adventure of your life. Whether or not you believe it to be true, it is. Over time, you will become more than you ever expected and will experience wonders not yet conceived. Knowledge can be limited, unless it is shared with and cultivated by others. So, grow from giving and allow the garden to become a paradise within you. Fulfill your purpose and remember: you have made it this far; I believe in you.

This is the doorway to completion. You don't have to take my word for it ... find out for yourself.

Good journeys,
Eric Pepin

Chapter 1

TIES THAT BIND

LOOK AT YOUR hand, what do you see? Now, go look at yourself in the mirror and ask the same question. What do you see? Do you see *you*? When you think of the body, do you see only one thing, *you*? Is it actually you?

If we look closely we may see a whole micro-universe of living cells and organisms. Every cell of our bodies is a unique, living creature, operating and functioning without our involvement. In fact, there is no physical *you*.

What we perceive to be ourselves is actually millions and trillions of living organisms, working with us in a shared relationship.

If I am not the cells or organisms then who am I?

If we removed all the cells and organisms that make up our bodies, what is left? The real essence of who we are is what remains.

Energy; we are beings made of energy. Think about it; when we touch a cold glass of water, the cells in our fingers send electrical signals through our nervous systems, into our brains, where the electricity is converted into the experience of touch.

Did we actually touch the glass? Isn't our experience of it shared with us through electricity? If no physical part of us touched the glass, it was a separate living organism. Part of us felt the experience; the energy part. Electricity equals energy in this case.

Ask yourself: what connects each of us to this world? Our five senses interpret what we see, smell, touch, taste, and hear and they primarily give each of us information through electricity. They are part of our organic bodies, which we need to interpret this physical dimension of solid matter.

What does 'the physical body interprets this dimension' mean? Doesn't the body experience it in a physical way?

At this exact moment, we are surrounded by cellular telephone frequencies, radio and television signals, wireless bandwidth, and all kinds of invisible transmissions passing through the atmosphere. Yet, we cannot experience this information, even though it surrounds each of us.

Why not? Because we need the right device to convert these signals to experience the information. Using a television, suddenly the invisible is visible. With a radio, sound is activated. A cellular telephone connects each of us to a vast, global communication grid. Without these mechanisms, the data essentially does not exist for us.

The physical world does not exist for an energy being. These beings have no eyes to see, ears to hear, or hands to touch. They need a physical body—the correct device—to interpret and experience it.

The five senses operate contrary to radios or cellular telephones. Rather than converting energy into the physical, they change the physical into energy, so energy beings (we) can experience it.

When ancient yogis, spiritual teachers, talk about a spiritual reality, what do they mean? Do you believe it to be a physical reality, much like this one, except somewhere else?

Somewhere you can physically travel? Is it a planet, galaxy, or some floating castle in the sky?

I am being a little sarcastic, but you get the point. If a spiritual reality isn't physical, how do we experience it?

When we think of spiritual, do we not perceive something more ethereal and less physical, energy-like? If it is not an actual place, but an invisible dimension, energetic frequency, how do we awaken and experience this energy reality?

This is the journey we will take, delving into these reality secrets. To remove the beliefs that have trapped us, such as who we really are, what dimensional consciousness is, and how to experience it. It is time to discover ourselves.

How long does this take? Where do I begin?

Realize awakening is a gradual process. Don't be in a rush. Slow down.

As you work use the techniques and knowledge in this book, the way you experience life will become clearer. Over time you begin to view life as qualities of energy and vibration, but even more so, you begin to understand there is something beyond. As you continue to apply these techniques, you will feel the presence of the universe envelop you.

At first it will be soft and subtle. When you hear music, birds, or a friend's voice, these sounds will become beautiful music playing in your head; singing through your being.

You will become aware the energy of the universe is one with all things; there is a difference between understanding this principle and experiencing it. I want you to experience it. Life becomes more rewarding and fulfilling when you understand it more deeply and become one with it.

You say energy is one with all things, yet, you say I am an energy being. What is this energy? How does it work?

When we embrace our true nature as energy beings, or begin to tap into dimensional frequency, we must first grasp the meaning of energy: what it is, how it affects us, and how to work with it. Spiritual energy, psychic energy, metaphysical energy actually controls, manipulates, and directs us every single day—99.9 percent of people have no idea they are being affected by it.

Each human being has an energy field called the aura. If you aren't able to see the aura, please know it's possible using information that walks you through it.

The human aura most people see is roughly radiating off the body anywhere from an inch to a couple inches. For me and other trained people, who see further levels of aura energy, it can extend up to thirty-two feet away.

When we walk into a room, our energy field (aura) already feels and touches every object in the environment. All of these objects hold a vibration programmed by intelligent living beings. This is done usually through broadcasting emotion because we have thirty-two feet of energy.

Whenever we are happy, depressed, or angry we're broadcasting this energy out as a frequency. Naturally, objects don't have an intellect to choose what to absorb from each of us, so they absorb whatever we send out. They accumulate energy and begin to bounce it back off or radiate it back out.

Imagine a sponge; we can only fill the sponge with so much liquid before it swells and drains. Well, if we're constantly emanating energy, every object in the environment is absorbing it until they get to a critical point where they can't absorb it anymore. So, they cast it out.

When you learn to see auras you'll find not only do human beings, plants, and animals have auras, but inanimate objects such beds, couches, countertops, and walls have auras as well.

You will be able see a very unique or defined level of energy emitting from them.

For example, say you go over to a friend's house and when you walk into the house you know instantly if you like being there or not. It's a kind of sense—you either feel comfortable or uncomfortable. It doesn't matter how clean or pretty the house is, you simply like it or don't.

You could go to a very dirty and messy house with tons of clothes scattered about and feel absolutely comfortable. You may go to another house where everything is pristine, bright, and shiny with flowers everywhere, yet you feel uncomfortable. It's because of the energy in the environment. It's programmed; people who live in a house, program the environment.

How does the energy become programmed?

Imagine you're in your house watching television, feeling very upbeat. You're in a very good mood; everything's fine. You hear a knock on the door; a friend comes to visit. Your friend is extremely angry and starts venting. He/She sits on your couch and grabs a pillow to hug as they talk to you, telling you about how angry they are about their employer, rent, or house problems. Your guest continues to complain about a relationship then takes the pillow and smashes it as they explain how they feel.

In frustration, your visitor eventually says, "Well, I've had enough, I'm done. I'm out of here." then gets up and storms out the door. You think: *okay, I wish I had been more supportive, but he/she needs to get over it. I'm sure we'll talk again.*

A few minutes later, you have another guest come over. This person comes in extremely happy and tells you what a wonderful day they had, what wonderful people they met, and how brilliantly things are going on. A completely opposite experience.

Your guest walks over and sits down on the same couch your angry friend sat on, picks up the same pillow, and hugs while talking to you. They share all the wonderful things happening in their life. After ten to fifteen minutes their tone of communication begins to change.

The person turns around and says something to the effect, "Are you listening to me because if you don't want to hear this right now, I can just leave."

You respond, "No, no, I'm ready to hear this."

"Well you don't seem like you're really into this, so I'm just going to leave. I'll talk to you later. Goodbye." They conclude and he leaves.

What happened? Why did their mood suddenly change?

Now, each of us at some point have had an experience like this in our lives. However, we never pay attention to what's going on or the details.

You may say," Well, I know that pillow had something to do with it."

That's exactly right. The first person came in, sat down on the couch, took the pillow and it became the focal point of their emotion. A pillow absorbs energy, but it doesn't know good, bad, or indifference; it's just a pillow.

As this same person was hitting the pillow, breathing his/her consciousness near the pillow, and emotionally raising and lowering his/her energies this pillow was saturated and programmed with these emotions. Anger, frustration, anxiety—all of these feelings were saturated like a sponge. Similar to injecting ink into a sponge. The pillow emanated or glowed in a sense, this vibration.

The next person who comes in, sits down, and picks up the pillow to hold it, his/her positive mood is affected. Negative energy tends to be stronger or more dominant than positive energy.

Think of negative as pushing someone, and positive as hugging someone. It's two different kinds of energies and intents. As soon as this person picks up and holds the pillow, it begins to push what saturates it into their energy field. Now, this person is not conscious about energy. They are not aware of being affected or that their mood may be manipulated by objects or furniture. Who would think of such a thing?

The brain, or at least the part that's trained, is never alerted about something that may be troubling. What happens is the brain, being a machine, receives signals that create a hyperventilation in the body and, perhaps, releases certain endorphins associated with muscle tension, frustration, anger. All the alarms for creating this effect start a chain reaction within the person.

Now, the person is intellectually focused on the conversation with you. What begins to happen is they start feeling anxiety, but don't know why. The visitor associates they must be angry and begins to automate and look for the root of this anger. There's nothing obvious to make them angry, so it must be you.

You, who the person is talking to, must be upsetting them somehow. So, now your visitor begins to look for a reason to argue.

They ask: "Why are you doing something to me? Why are you not listening to me?"

It's similar to the brain and intellect meeting at a fifty-fifty point because biochemically you're reacting to this energy from this pillow. You assume there's a problem and create a problem by attacking basically yourself, or this person is going to attack you because they think you're being negative.

However, it's really the energy from the pillow that's making them feel this way; they just don't know it. So, the person leaves, but the pillow was programmed.

Now, let's talk about programming. Our bodies have an energy field; we emanate it. We can detect it basically when we see auras, Kirlian photography—there are various ways.

We know energy moves through our bodies: our hearts beat to it; our liver and kidneys communicate through our brains. There are low radiation impulses, electrons, and various functions. Our entire bodies are an electrical field that makes everything communicate and function. So, we have this vast energy field that is not only internal, but external. We don't pay much attention to how much actually works, which we'll cover soon.

We are thinking creatures. Human beings are very mentally, intelligently willful; we can project our thoughts in different ways. When a human being picks up an object or touches it, we can create emotions in them and project them; it's like pushing into something.

We can literally touch it and will a certain emotion or feeling we create inside—like an inner-development—and we push it out as if we're projecting it into an object. In many cases, it's not even that we're pushing energy outside of ourselves, we are programming or telling it what it's going to do.

A piece of furniture will absorb light from your room. It will absorb heat and music from the room. Music doesn't echo through the room. Light doesn't reflect like it's hitting mirrors. Everything is being absorbed; energy is just transferred and being created into something else.

Objects don't have bad or good intentions, they just exist. However, they're radiating this energy because like a sponge they can only absorb so much light, sound, or heat before they begin to project it out.

When a human picks up that same object, it's like a chalkboard. It's not a wall; it's a chalkboard, saying, "I am ready to be written on. I have the resources; I am made of slate. I am prepared for you to write on me."

A carpet or a piece of cloth is not designed to be written on. So, an object that absorbs energy that doesn't have intent—any message, any programming just light energy, heat, sound—is waiting to be transfigured.

When a person actually touches an object, they can literally create or write a message like on a chalkboard and program it into the object. Therefore, when another person touches the same object, or creature for that matter, they absorb the message that was programmed.

If I held a rock programmed for positive, happy energy, could I feel that happy energy?

We receive the message that's encoded. Our brains decode it. Most of the time it's a very unconscious act; people aren't aware these things affect them. The same way there are radio signals transmitting right now, we can't hear or see them. We don't really know they exist. Does it mean they don't exist? No, they're everywhere. Same thing with cellular telephones, wireless internet, and everything else.

Think about it, there's a mass amount of information all around us going on we can't see, hear, or feel. A device doesn't exist to capture information then recreate and show it to us on a level we can understand.

Let's go back to the rock programmed with positive energy. It is possible to program the rock beyond a simple emotion. You could program it with knowledge, or a message you want the person to know. The rock is programmed, but by looking at it we wouldn't know there is a message contained within. When we actually touch or feel it, our brains decode the message as an emotion, not words.

We're not going to hear a story or a conversation instructing, "Okay, take a left at the next tree." It's more of an emotion, which is a universal language. So, this object can communicate with us, we just don't realize how it's communicating.

Everything in life has these energies and programs in them. They're constantly being built then destroyed, rebuilt then destroyed, or they wear away and refill. You may think: *how does this happen?*

Well, let's say we program a stone with energy, but we leave it in the sun. As the sun pounds the stone with its energy, eventually it resembles a sponge.

Let's say we pour red dye into a sponge then start to pour milk into it. Eventually the color will turn dark red as its being refilled. Then it slowly turns pink. The pink coloring takes on a very faint red tint in the white milk then eventually pushes it all out until its white milk again.

All objects have an exchange of energy, depending on the circumstances of their environment. Objects in a home tend to maintain the vibration longer because they constantly feed off the person, who reproduces the mentality or emotion in their environment.

How does all of this affect me?

When we walk into someone's house, we can feel their house the same way we can feel a person with our energy field. Let's say we're at a party, restaurant, or somewhere in an environment where there are a lot of people. On one level we have absorbed the frequencies of the people around us.

We begin to feel comfortable, so we start to have a conversation with someone and get into the zone of whatever we're doing. However, all of the sudden our sensory says, "Hey look behind you." We feel an impulse to look.

So, we turn around to look and there's someone coming through the doorway, maybe thirty feet away or so. We instantly know whether we like or dislike the person, or perceive this person as a threat or non-threat.

Do you even care? There is something going on as far as communication between us and the person; that's energy.

It's similar to an energy transference, like data between two computers. Although, mentally we're not actively thinking, we internalize a sense of making a decision. We simply aren't fully aware we are, or paying particular attention to the fact we are.

Your thirty-two foot field of energy meets their thirty-two foot field, making sixty-four feet. It's a very large distance to feel things.

When we're in a house, we *feel* the environment. When we are driving through a town, we will *feel* that town.

We'll intuitively know we don't want to be there, or there's something very unpleasant or unlikable about the particular town we are passing through.

As we move through the town or head out the other side of the town, we feel alleviated. Almost like, "Okay, I feel better now. I'm not in that area or vibration any longer."

There's always a store in every city where no matter what business moves into that building, it fails. A McDonald's can open in the same location and it may survive because its brand is iconic, but it'll be the worst McDonald's with the least amount of business.

The energy of that environment is programmed into it. In this particular case, it may be something emanating from the ground, mineral pressurization, or frequencies emitting that we are unaware we are feeling. Somehow, these energies are communicating to us no matter how good the food, service, or lighting and structure of this environment is.

Something within us is thinking: *I'm not happy here and I don't want to come here again.* We're constantly influenced by these energies, the same thing about driving through the town. Other towns we travel to feel really good; we like the environment. These places align with our energy field. So, we make decisions without realizing we're making them.

Experiencing and understanding energy is very interesting because we do it all the time.

Have you ever worn a friend's clothes and felt your friend's energy for a few moments? As if you could *feel* them then after a few moments the feeling fades away and the clothing becomes part of you?

It's your friend's energy on the article of clothing; your energy as the dominant will begin to have the same effect of the sponge. You're going to push your friend's energy out and eventually dominate the clothing until it takes on all of your energy.

So, it's very interesting when we pick up objects, we can feel the other person's presence, vibration, or energy on them.

There are people, who have had arguments and come to me for counseling. Their relationship was on its way out, they were headed for divorce, or they had severe problems. They're always thrown a little off with some of the questions posed because they probably think my focus will on their relationship problems.

Instead, I asked, "Do you argue while you're driving together?"

They respond, "No."

"Do you argue or have problems while you're at home?"

"Yeah."

"Where do you find these problems occur?"

"Well, all over."

"If you had to pick an area in your home, where would it be?"

In this particular case, we narrowed it down to the kitchen. They would come home, be in the kitchen, each do their own thing then start to nit pick:

"You're in my space. Can't you give me some space when I get home from work?"

"Well, I work and I'm tired, too."

An argument would escalate and feed, they created this bitter fight, and marched off into other parts of the house, slamming doors. My summation—to make it quick and to the point—was at some point they had an intense argument, which took place in the kitchen.

Each slamming his/her hand on the counter and refrigerator door, or placing his/her hand on the refrigerator door while yelling at the other in the corner of the kitchen. A volley of negative energy impacted this kitchen so powerfully, it became the dominant energy.

Once our bodies are exhausted, we either shut down and go to sleep or go do something. We don't remain in argument mode if the energy is affecting us. There's an exhaustive point when we become worn out and step away from this zone.

What happens is this couple would come home, go into the kitchen, and find they consistently felt this *need* of irritation as if the other person's very presence was annoying them. The bickering would start then escalate into an argument.

So, I would ask, "Do you fight on the way home?"

They answered, "Well, no."

"Do you fight while you undress, change to unwind?"

"No."

"Do you sometimes go into the living room before you enter the kitchen?"

"Yeah, sometimes we'll bring home food to eat."

"Do you fight then?"

"Well, no."

"However, you do fight. Do you do it while you're in the kitchen?"

"Well, yeah."

Then they started to figure it out.

Again, what happens is similar to the pillow mentioned earlier. They enter a room—the kitchen—and they're in perfectly fine moods; they're very compatible. Soon, the energy in the room is so powerful it begins to affect them, creating the endorphin release in their brains. Their brains are reacting to what they are feeling.

Instead of seeing it with our eyes, we react to it. When we hear a baby cry, we have a natural sense that reacts to this sound. When we hear a woman scream for help, we have a natural sense that reacts to this sound. If we see fire, we know we better react to it. These are all feelings and emotions also associated with these things.

Well, this couple's kitchen had an intense negative energy. They felt it and began to find reasons to argue. They began to look for the reason why they felt the way they felt. So, the energy dominated their situation.

Naturally, I'm often asked what we can do to change this scenario. Can we fix it? Can we resolve this problem? The answer is *yes*. A kitchen is much more difficult to work with, but it's possible. I'll share with you a simpler example.

In the tradition of Feng Shui, which is an ancient Chinese system of aesthetics developed over three thousand years ago, the idea that if we place certain objects in certain areas, it facilitates a fluidity of energy. Have you ever re-arranged your bedroom or moved the bed? You felt the need to change it.

When you changed it, it felt better, as if something had been lifted out of the room. We think: *ahh, this works for me.*

What we've done is break the pattern of energy in the bedroom—the best way to deal with negative energy in a home setting. Energy begins in the pillow I was talking about earlier. Left alone, the couch doesn't have good or bad intentions; it's simply another chalkboard. This pillow has a very powerful program in it, similar to a virus that begins to seep into other pillows and the couch it rests upon.

The same way a sponge would infiltrate other sponges if constantly filled with the red dye when the remainder are only filled with milk, we'd eventually see a flow of pink come from every sponge by the end of the night. In the same way, this energy dominates other pillows. It starts to dominate the couch, other chairs, floor, and walls. It spreads similar to how fungus or a virus would spread, it's a natural process.

Over time, it starts to dominate the energy in an environment. This is when the chaos and negativity begin to change. The only way we're going to stop this domination from happening is to understand energy seems to have vibrational patterns. It always follows specific sequences.

Energy is extremely organized; it has a predetermined course. The best way to cut its advancement is to begin reconfiguring all the furniture in an environment. When we move furniture, energy collapses. Similar to a cake being baked in the oven, at a certain point, if we slam the oven door, it collapses because it hasn't solidified to support itself.

If we move the couch, we move the furniture, we change the entire room, and energy loses its linkage to how it established itself to build its vibrational pattern in the room. It has become very weak. We haven't destroyed it 100 percent, but we've weakened it greatly. It will take a lot of time for it to come back.

In the meantime, we want to start projecting positive energy in the room. We can find some really good music we enjoy—tunes that evoke a very positive mood—then sit down on our couches to reflect on wonderful beautiful thoughts and almost breathe them in and back out.

We breathe out to project this energy into the couch, our environment, and into the walls. We need to see ourselves filling the entire room with positive energy we're feeling from, perhaps, the inducement of great music, which will wipe out all of the bad programming in the room.

We're going to directly affect and change it, and it's the same way with the bedroom. Usually what happens without realizing it, people tend to move furniture around to put them in a good mood. Their positive mood now begins to be the dominant programming in the room, which indirectly rids remnants of the negative energy.

Do you have to be spiritual to feel this energy?

Many people naturally sense these kinds of energies— they have eccentric cleaning or arranging dispositions, and feel they have to clean or move things around constantly. They're not foolish; they really sense something. This is a natural instinct.

The same way a person, who is underwater and wants to breathe, or the way we feel hunger, it's an instinct. They know instinctively something is wrong with the environment; it's willing itself in a way they can feel.

Unconsciously the mind automatically has an under-standing it needs to do things. In many cases, this is the reason why people feel an overwhelming desire to change their bedrooms. Our minds are the most consciously open while in our bedrooms because this is where we sleep; therefore, this room is where we first feel the need to maybe change things.

Simplicity keeps the mind from being too attached in one spiritual aspect. Conversely, bad energy is always looking for something to build upon.

If you have a pile of clothes in the room, it will grow like mold; it has something to hang onto. If you've got a bunch of paper magazines piled up, it will grow because it has something to cling to. If you have a wide open room filled with very simple things—perhaps a bed and one bureau with nothing else in it—it is very difficult for energy to compound itself.

Long surfaces such as a floor seem to stretch or thin energy out before it can gain enough strength, before it can move to the next object or area to penetrate. Consequently, having a very neat and tidy environment is an asset to controlling the energy of an environment; it has very little to build upon.

The other tool we may use has been around for thousands of years; many spiritualists have used it, *salt*. We know salt is a cleansing agent, a purifier. Salt, when used in a room, collapses the energy. I have advised couples experiencing relationship problems to sprinkle salt all over their floor; not huge quantities or piles. Sprinkle it all over the place and leave it overnight to control the energy level within their homes.

How does salt rid energy? It doesn't quite make sense. The truth to the matter is, there are physical elements we have yet to understand. However, it works as sure as the sun shines light; it works.

Salt takes energy—it's indifferent, neutral. It doesn't matter whether it's good or bad energy; it's a giant eraser for a chalkboard. It takes negative and positive information and cleans it away, removing it.

It doesn't destroy the energy because energy can't really be destroyed, but salt removes the programming in it. Similarly, it's like a magnet to a computer disk, it pulls data right off of it, but leaves the material. So, salt is a wonderful environmental cleanser.

I counseled a couple, who had serious problems and received the same information being shared in this book. They actually went as far as to wash the walls with salt water, also.

It greatly contributed to saving their marriage. Not only that, but they felt there were a lot of bad vibrations in the house. From spirits to entities to people, who lived there before and programmed their home.

The bad vibrations always seemed to resurface; after washing the walls with salt, this couple said it was the first time in the few years they had lived there when they felt it was clean, like a brand new house feels. Again, an inner-sense that knows when something is new.

Their relationship was very bad, I mean they were actually having physical fights with each other. There was alcohol abuse coupled with their aggressive arguments and fighting. Literally within a matter of days they began to experience a whole new relationship; a cooling down in that area.

Theirs became a very positive relationship as time progressed. The big contributor to this relational shift was the salt, moving the furniture around, and acknowledging and thinking about how energy affects them. By adopting these three tools, we can literally change how we're affected in life. Additional examples of how an environment affects us include meditation to reduce our thought activity and constant babbling. During meditation, we can experience total silence. Afterwards, we can begin to think and communicate more clearly about running errands, shopping, yard work, or doing laundry.

Is a Babbler influenced by outside energy?

The real question is: are there any outside forces in our rooms that constantly bombard us with energy? Of course, we're constantly bombarded by the Gaia Consciousness, a more conscious way of working with our inner-resources.

This means all living beings are thinking and because we're all thinking we're broadcasting, like radio towers, tele-pathic consciousness, emotions, and feelings. So, if we live in an urban environment, our thinking is more intense. If we live in the country, our thoughts are not quite as intense, but much calmer.

When we meditate in the city dwelling, we find we really need discipline and focus to really get ourselves to the right zone to experience the best mediation. It is ironic when people don't always recognize this need.

If we travel to the country, a state park, or to the forest then we meditate or spend the day in one of these alternate environments, our minds become very quiet. We become very calm. It's almost as if we feel very sleepy at the end of the day.

We prepare for deep rest because everything has seemingly been released from our inner-muscles and bodies. This is largely because there's no willful energy or vibrations being imposed on us such as in people's houses, at work, the store, and everywhere else.

We must remember that nature, more specifically, trees, are living things, and as stated previously, they do have a very simple intelligence. They want to live, thrive, and grow. They nourish and give forth life and fruit, wanting to propagate life.

When we go into nature, negative forces can't dominate us, at least from a human level, because anything a human may do—with negative energy that could impact the stones on the ground—within a day, the greater force from trees, which is the dominant energy being pushed out, is going to wash away all bad vibrations.

It's like constantly pouring fresh milk into a sponge; no matter what drops on the sponge, it never ceases pouring milk. Eventually, it keeps flushing whatever was dropped into it away.

When we go into nature, it's always a healing, good experience. It's a great place if we're having trouble restricting thoughts during meditations. If we want to give ourselves an advantage, we can go out and meditate in the park, a state park, or rent a cabin using the system shared later in this book.

We will almost double or triple the effects of our meditation by doing this. It lifts a huge weight off us like a backpack we're trying to carry. Our technique is good; it's designed for high stress. So, it's going to work one way or another. It's more advantageous if we are able to venture into nature occasionally.

This is why natural environments, in terms of energy, are much better than in urban areas. In the city, there are millions of programmed energies bombarding us constantly.

Let's talk about energy, more specifically spiritualists who use magic, prayer, or a variety of other things. An interesting thing about energy that doesn't initially occur to most people when they learn this information, is that we can do magic if we choose to, understanding this knowledge.

What do I mean by this? Let's imagine the same pillow the person deposited bad energy into. If we could take a pillow and hold it in our arms—thinking of love and happiness—we could really fill it with this energy.

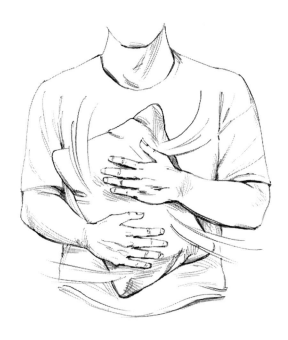

Objects can be programmed by moving your energy into them.

We can breathe in then out from our bodies into this pillow, these very emotions. Of course, the more our minds remain on these emotions, the better the experience is going to be.

We could literally program the pillow to have this wonderful positive energy and give it to someone we care about as a gift; someone, who is ill or not feeling well; or a grandparent who is having problems. What a wonderful gift to offer!

We can also help people who are sick by giving them enhanced healing energy. The possibilities of what we can program are only limited by our imaginations. Do you understand?

Yes. We can willfully use our energy to program objects for specific purposes.

If we wanted to do something wonderful, we can. When I was younger, I studied a significant amount about magic. I often thought: *if there's a truth to magic, what is the science behind it?*

The science behind magic is: anybody who performs magic whether it be pagan, African, Norwegian, or Nordic rune magic; shamanism; or anything else, it's a recipe to seduce us into a certain state-of-consciousness. It's designed to clear our minds.

All of this really is not the secret to what makes magic work or the projection of thought. It is the recipe, which entices us into the right state-of-mind to do the best work. It calms us so we're not thinking about what is happening in our lives, then finally suggests in the recipe for us to now hold the pillow.

With these final words, what is being suggested is the pillow will now make us happy and prosperous in our lives. What we're really doing is believing we're creating an emotion to project into this pillow.

If we throw magic out the window, along with the incantations, recipes, and whatever is used during our meditation, which is purely and infinitely more powerful because we're trained to have clear thought, we're now trained to have focus.

To a certain degree, we've worked to remove the Babbler and we project this energy into this object. We've now created—what would be called in ancient times—a very powerful, magical item. This, of course, leads to many possibilities; we can do good and bad.

Once a friend came to me, who owned a duplex many years ago. His tenants weren't paying their rent and he couldn't get them evicted. They were apparently destroying the place and he really didn't have a lot of money for repairs.

He asked, "What am I going to do?"

So, I gave him the following lesson I'm going to share with you now. I instructed him to take their floor mat in the middle of the night.

I advised my friend to earnestly project the following thoughts into their floor mat, "Move! Leave! You would be happier somewhere else. You need to go."

I explained to him when he was done speaking these words and felt he'd done a good job understanding everything I'd taught him, just leave the mat there.

He did this. Approximately one or two weeks later, his tenants told him they were moving and asked if he wanted it in writing. They were prepared to give him whatever he needed. He could not believe they decided to move.

It could have been coincidence, it could have been chance, it could have been anything, but what are the chances of this being so coincidental? I can disclose hundreds of stories like this. It may be said our magic is as good as our will and clarity to project it into an item, and how much we're willing to clearly project into it.

This is how certain spiritual items were created by ancestors who had spiritual beliefs. Whether they be amulets, objects of protection, worn around the neck; tokens; a wood staff; etcetera. Spiritual people projected what they believed was magic will into these things, giving them a life of their own, a meaning that was a program in our modern day thinking. That's what they did.

We as energy beings can take a necklace and project absolute love into the necklace then give it to someone to wear. It's no different than a priest blessing an item or a shaman performing ritual blessings. They don't put much thought into it. The majority of spiritual people, who do the more ritualistic consider it a job; it's more a show to demonstrate these things are done.

The secret and quality of what we're doing is going to rely upon how well our minds can be focused and project from a very emotional place, the data we're going to project into an object. That's the secret.

It's only for these few moments we have a very clear and defined message to project into whatever object we want. We can do good and bad, and of course, always want to keep an eye for people, who would do something bad with such objects.

Another perspective of energy is in the psychic arena. There is a level of programs that can be put out. On a minor level, people sense an environment and know if it feels good or bad; or somebody coming into a room, whether they like the individual or not, or feel the clothing energy from a person.

A psychic who's more evolved or practiced now can be more defined about energy. They can acquire more information. The same way that our brains interpret emotional energy, a trained psychic can actually get more information.

Instead of it making the person upset, or angry, or feel emotions, they can actually decipher more information. Instead of it being a television that captures radio signals, maybe we don't have an image, just audio.

A psychic gets the audio as well as images at the same time, whereas other people are more limited. A psychic may get images from a building—they may see things that have happened, traumatic things, because disturbing things tend to broadcast stronger and more intensely. It burns a greater image into objects, so the psychic feels it.

A psychic may see the images and in some cases, feel what somebody feels, something touching their throat, or squeezing their throat, making breathing harder because the data is broadcasting a signal. Not only is their mind seeing it, but their body is reacting to what this person reacted to because it's a message.

It's a program and our bodies react the same way we hold a programmed pillow and our blood pressure increases, endorphins release, and we feel anger or tension in our bodies. For a psychic, they're getting a greater visual and feeling, perhaps a choking sensation or heaviness in breathing.

So, they use this data to interpret within themselves. They use their entire bodies to interpret the message of what's going on rather than simply feeling the base emotions of something.

Psychics also get impressions from energy, but they get another level, a higher level. Again the reason is negativity tends to be what these people pick up. Mainly because it's the strongest broadcast in most cases, not all cases, but most cases. Of course, the stronger the psychic, the more defined they can pick up on the littler things undetectable by others.

They have a better senses, per se, and can acquire better information, depending on how much they practice. Of course, anybody, who uses techniques we provide will eventually reach these levels, if they work on them.

**When you worked to find missing people, you held objects belonging to people.
Is it because of this energy? The psychic impressions?**

This is the very reason; their frequency is embedded or imbued into the objects they wear. It's the same as when we wear a friend's article of clothing, we feel their vibration.

Every human being has a very specific frequency, much like a radio channel; no two human beings have the same.

When we tune into a person's radio frequency, there's a collective consciousness file on the person and we begin to gather information regarding their life, or who the person is, or what they are about.

On a case I worked in Florida fifteen to twenty years ago, I was able to get this information from an old pair of sneakers that had been wrapped. I held these sneakers, but couldn't get much information from them. I put a little bit of salt on the sneaker to agitate it. I had an instinct it may help me pick up a better impression. It was like putting a little battery to resurface data in the shoe.

Information, as worn out as it may be, may still resurface from objects. Metal holds information better than clothing or natural fibers.

If, in the future, you decide to start working on other areas of psychic development to be covered, please reference this class to identify the other areas. This is what connects most work psychically, which is called psychometry: a form of extrasensory perception. When objects are held, data is pulled from these objects—by their frequencies—so we have an understanding of them.

If energy can be projected into objects, can energy be projected into people, too?

If someone projects psychic energy directly at us rather than into an object, how do we protect ourselves? It is a form of psychic attack. Whether they are aware of it or not, it does not change what it is. Unless their intentions are good, which is how healing occurs.

Using energy to project into another person, is a lesson for another time. However, if it is a psychic attack, a quick, simple answer is to think about our lower chakra—a main energy center in our bodies. Our lower chakra is similar to chi for martial artists. It's the closest one to our physical bodies and energy.

Focusing on our lower chakra holds our energy in, so psychic attacks can't infiltrate our energy. If we want to counter such energy, we simply think about our heart chakra. The second we think about our heart chakra, should bring a smile across our faces.

As soon as we do this, it's like a white light burning into any brown or black energy coming at us. It's like light piercing through the darkness. It pushes a psychic attack away instead of letting it emanate and attach to us. Even if we have a lot of energy thrown on us that's really dark, negative, and hateful, when we sit down to meditate, it usually blows it all out.

However, if we simply want a quick focus right on our heart chakra, we breathe in then out to feel our heart chakra energy expanding. It instantly washes it right off us.

Many times when I entered a haunted house, I put my hand on a wall to project this energy to push all negative energy out. I focus my heart energy and go into my spiritual enlightened state. I think about my meditation and this beautiful place—feeling the Universe and opening up what I call the *dimensional rift*, where God is most brilliant.

Open the flood gates inside of you! It's like a dimming switch to a light. Out of darkness comes light radiating out. So, I project this energy outward then I push it into the walls, causing these walls to fill with this light.

It's the same way we would hold an object, except I have so much more energy to give, probably far more than most people. When someone emits or sends us negative energy, we should simply project positive energy outward.

There are more advanced techniques that allow us to control and program our energy more effectively. There are very unique things we can do to change our frequency to protect us against other energy or counter it.

These are very ancient teachings from thousands of years ago that have been lost. I want to reintegrate them because they're very powerful. I will share these techniques as this book progresses.

Chapter 2

FOUNDATION

WHAT YOU ARE about to experience is a profoundly new concept for entering higher consciousness. You will learn a technique that reaches beyond normal meditation as most people understand it. You will discover the missing link other schools of self-development either have no idea about, or simply will not share because it is assumed most people are not ready for it.

At some point in your life, you learned about the soul. It was explained when you die, this is who you really are. In the upcoming chapter, you will learn how the soul is actually another body similar to our physical bodies, but made of energy. When we touch or smell something, our physical bodies convert the experience into energy and our brains experience it for us.

Pay close attention to that last part. The brain experiences it for us. All electrical impulses from our senses are brought to, and experienced in, the brain. Yet the brain is not us, it is still sharing these experiences with us.

The brain is also physical, made of independent, living organisms. This fact begs the question: does the brain report to something higher? Yes, it does: the mind. The brain and mind are two separate, distinct places of consciousness.

The mind is not physical; it's made of energy and often considered to be the soul. As energy, the mind cannot experience the physical world, so it uses the organic body to explore and experience this dimension. Everything we touch, smell, taste, see, and hear is converted into energy for the mind.

When we attempt to experience a dimensional realm—God, the Universe, Prana, the Force; call it what you will—we try to do it using a physical body and an organic brain. We are using the wrong tool for the job. The brain has taken us far, but it has reached its limit or capabilities to interpret the level of consciousness we wish to understand.

Imagine a horse has carried you across the land to the ocean shore. Do you now expect the horse to take you across the ocean? Of course not, but this is exactly what we're doing when we use our physical brains and bodies to experience something spiritual. We must become familiar with this other energy body, to nourish it with energy and make it strong. Allow our energy minds to interface with this energy body, so its dimensional brain can interpret dimensional places and experiences for us, as our physical bodies and brains do for us here.

Foundation is designed to take complex knowledge and simplify it without losing a drop of critical knowledge. It uses simple analogies and concepts. It's not how we learn that's important; it's only important to understand it.

We will learn to think and communicate with our dimensional minds, learn to acquire the correct energy to feed our energy bodies, and master its ability to explore and experience higher dimensions much like our physical bodies do here.

The meditation, you will soon discover, is unlike other meditations. It will allow you to harmonize with the Universe and achieve great inner-peace. As this is being achieved during your meditation, you will attract energy, which nourishes your dimensional body.

As the dimensional body is nourished and gains strength, it gives a sense of completion to us as a whole being. It feels as if we have found the part of ourselves that was missing.

As a whole being, we gain other senses much like the five senses of our physical bodies, but rather, these are dimensional body senses. These senses allow us to interpret, communicate, integrate, and experience other dimensions.

I feel excited, but a little nervous. What if I'm not ready for all of these things, yet?

Naturally, each person controls their experience. In other words, the Universe unfolds no faster than we're prepared to experience it. So, if inner-peace is all we desire, this is where we will remain. If we desire more understanding of the Universe, or to directly experience, then it will unfold and share itself on profound levels.

This may seem difficult, but rest assured, years have gone into developing this system; anyone who invests a little time can and will achieve it. If you can understand what has been said, you will have no problem understanding the complete training course. This knowledge is the key to higher awareness. It will open all teachings that may have eluded you before.

Most people think of meditation in the most general way—it's a way of relaxation, feeling comfortable, or relieving stress. This is true; it is all of these things. More so, there are other profound areas of meditation.

Not only can it be used to relax, but it can be used to improve our mental abilities. Scholastically, if we were to read something or study, and had trouble finding an interest or maintaining our concentration on the subject, through meditation we'd learn to remain focused or allow information to flow through our minds easily.

Other meditation formats introduce ways to improve athletically, whether it be throwing a football or hitting a baseball. Martial artists have been aware of using meditation to remain focused on what they need to do in terms of: feeling pain, controlling pain, performing at a peak level, athletically;

using the mind to transcend pain, which distracts their concentration from an intended goal.

Other benefits of meditation include, but are not limited to: a sense of well-being; inner-communion; balanced health; being able to lower high blood pressure without medication, to a certain point; and being able to control various body chemicals that cause depression or anxiety. The ability to lower anxiety levels and change brain chemistry may be done through sheer will.

Every aspect of meditation has an extremely positive intent. There is nothing terribly negative about meditation in any way.

Now, there are master areas of meditation. People, who have taken meditation to levels previously discussed in this book, should consider there are ways to reach what we call higher states of consciousness. Once you've achieved these other levels, or find a usefulness you can apply, one begins to ask if you want to go deeper.

It's similar to going into a building then into a certain room that may have something you want to see. Once a person has absorbed what they have seen, this individual then decides they have received what was expected and now it's time to leave; however, they can return at will. On the other hand, a person may enter the building and simply ask, "What is behind these doors?"

What are the possibilities of what lies beyond? The bottom line is when we meditate, we become familiar with the space we're in; it becomes our zone, comfort place, place of sanctuary. At some point, we become aware of other doorways in this space, and we have to choose to approach them, open them, and see where they take us.

These other places are higher states of consciousness, which go beyond our normal means of thinking, understanding, or reflection. Possibly something profound that we've never thought of or experienced before—completely new to our senses. These are places where spiritualists, gurus, shamans, or spiritual masters have gone.

They have approached these doorways and gone through them. Instead of staying at the first level of relaxation and remaining there, they have mastered this ability and elevated it into a higher level, or a new level of awareness.

Then again, there are doorways that keep going further and deeper into the absolutely profound, whereby the teacher is mastering it so well, he's bringing back knowledge from these higher levels, trying to share this new-found knowledge with people, so they can have an idea of where it is they may take their exploration, or how to begin their discovery.

It's like trying to give a person a map, but the map is only so good. One has to experience the journey on their own.

Sometimes people ask, "What can meditation do for me?"

My response, "Why do we need meditation?" This response, in itself, answers what it can do.

One of the first realizations about humankind is we are a biological creature in most ways. Evolution has exponentially pushed us beyond all other species on this planet to the point we're driving cars, beeping horns, yelling out windows, watching extreme television and radio, and juggling a million different things in our lives.

We have social stresses to provide financially and be positioned at certain places at certain times while dealing with a daily crisis. Comparatively, our ancestors (thousands of years ago) worried about where we're going to find food or shelter, or whether or not an animal was going to approach them. For the most part, the majority of life during their era was serene.

Humankind was very nomadic, so as a clan in primitive times, they walked stretches of the earth then found places to settle. Our ancestors had a significant amount of time to reflect and would go to the edge of water and sit. What was going through their minds? They didn't have all of the demands of everyday life as we know it on their minds.

They had simple thoughts as they watched water fall from a brook to hit the water's base. As they watched leaves glide down a stream, they settled into a very clear, stasis, and relaxed state of mind. Our forefathers were mentally entrenched in these activities because they didn't have to deal with the complexities we deal with now.

Our ancestors walked through a forest and looked at the canopy of trees—filled with life from the sun—emerald green with traces of golden light silently dancing on the ground. They found it effortless to ease into a very meditative, relaxed state of mind.

So, nature was humankind's first teacher. Nature was our first gift to receive and be transported into a very serene state of mind. We were predestined to have stresses; we may argue with other people in our social unit, or lose a child, etcetera. We certainly experienced stress, but we could equally find contentment in serene moments.

We're considerably drawn to water movement as a species. Why is there such an appeal towards water for humans? One aspect, and certainly not completely the only truth, is the shimmering and reflective property of water causes us to reflect.

This was the first mirror. When primitive man looked into water, it was the first time they actually saw themselves. We had to have asked: Is this all I am? Is this reflection who I am? Is it from this being I see this place my sight comes from—is this who I am?

It began what I refer to as the first reflection of creating a soul. Inner-reflection facilitates the awakening of our souls. It's energy takes on a shape or body within us.

Meditation developed from this place, and at some point we became more evolved and became more entrenched in life. Our brains became bigger to take on more tasks to think about and more things to reflect upon.

Some of us realized there was a place where our minds could go. We started to purposely place ourselves in this state to reap the rewards of feeling calmness. The discovery of what we deem *meditation* was now put into a systematic approach.

Rather than us stumbling into this state of mind in our primitive state, we now acknowledge there is a state of consciousness we choose to find.

It seems people still experience and seek out meditation, they just don't realize it.

The irony is people who never meditate or use a system of meditation, and say they don't meditate and don't know what it is, seek out meditation their whole life! For example, every time we go to a park, why *are* we going to the park? We go to the park to find some solitude or peace in our lives. This is a form of meditation.

Some people prefer to listen to music, which takes them into a meditative state while others cook. Cooking puts them in a meditative state. So, we really must ask ourselves: what puts me in a meditative state? Taking our minds off something less desirable distracts our minds. So, we have learned to indirectly remove ourselves from stresses in order to find some inner-peace.

Well, this is what meditation is in the end. We are removing ourselves willfully by simply sitting down and applying the technique, more so than saying we are going to listen to music or paint a painting.

Now, what we consciously have is a system easier to approach with, perhaps, a larger goal in mind, and more flexibility about what is being offered than a simplistic meditation level. Make no mistake about it, all of these things in life we naturally seek out without realizing it is, indeed, meditation.

Going for a walk is considered meditation. Most people don't go for a walk simply for their health. They go because it clears their minds; it loosens blockages. Back in primitive times, our ancestors walked everywhere. As they walked, their minds were so empty there was a sereneness. Experiencing life, the energies of life and nature were where we really learned to find inner peace.

It is now a matter of finding ways to apply it in the modern age, so we can acquire it more easily, or in doses we need more so now than in the more simplistic ways we found it. Again, there is a level of meditation.

Most people, who approach meditation say they are not really interested in reaching or speaking to other beings, or finding higher enlightenment. They are afraid of meditation, afraid it may infringe upon their religious beliefs.

I would advise such a person to work at meditation and master it. We can go to that place whenever we want to; there is no need to go any further. We can do meditations to find the deep relaxation we want; learn to relax; let go of problems, issues, and stresses; and be at peace within.

This approach helps to heal our bodies. It brings us balance, hence, higher balance. *Higher* is to say there are places we can go beyond relaxation and simply letting go.

When you're ready, you can move on to a second level, which is what I call *the planes of light*. The planes of light are vibrations or energies that exist beyond this tonal.

Imagine you're in a car on a a six-lane highway and you're in the slowest moving lane. The car is traveling at forty miles per hour. I am driving and there are cars passing by in the other lanes.

I look over at you and say, "Hey, what is the passenger reading in that other car? I thought I saw a magazine in his hand."

You respond, "Well, how am I supposed to know? They just flew past us."

The lane we're traveling in is *this* dimension. It's vibrating; everything is made of energy, including the chair you're sitting on. Everything is molecular energy when we really understand physics. We need to move up to a higher dimension in order to experience that dimension.

So, we step on the gas, speed up, and move from forty to sixty miles per hour. Once we're at 60 miles per hour, driving along the side of the next car, I say to you, "Well, what are they reading? Do you know, now?"

Your response, "Sure, they are reading such-and-such magazine and looking at blah, blah, blah."

If you can grasp the concept, you no longer relate so much to what we were doing at forty miles per hour because we have stepped out of that frequency. We're in a different frequency.

So, now I ask, "What are they reading or what are they doing in the car beyond that?"

You answer, "Well, hang on."

Now that you understand frequencies, you're going to move us now from sixty to eighty miles per hour and we're going to drive alongside that car.

You continue, "Well, their interior is made out of leather, and there is a lady in the backseat. I like the particular necklace she's wearing,"

You can experience that higher frequency now.

However, if I say to you, "So, what's happening now back in our old dimension?"

You're going to say, "I don't know. We're going to have to slow down."

So, we slow the gearing down and drop into lanes until we are eventually in the slower lane.

When we meditate, there are doorways, or other levels, we learn to approach. We cannot approach these levels until we have first mastered each one. In other words, we cannot go to the planes of light if we have not learned to relax in the first level.

If we have learned to relax ourselves, we can attain the frequency. As we have mastered it, we have learned to master the frequency that allows us to now move by will into the next lane, next level. Then we can experience what's there; we can understand what's there and find what is useful to our future development.

Once we have mastered that environment, that lane then we use these skills to move into the next lane, the next doorway, then we can experience what's there. Each lane holds something more profound than the last one.

Please understand, these lanes are infinite in some ways. Now, if you are a spiritual person, it is not being taught that you go to God's house by flying a rocket to heaven, but rather heaven surrounds us. We have forgotten how to experience or approach it, or to say heaven really is God. God is everywhere.

In order for us to really experience God, we should cease talking at God saying what we need. We must sit and simply listen, internalize and remove all thoughts, calm our minds then allow God to approach us in such a way that we say we're ready to listen.

God then moves us, or we move into higher lanes, and if we enter the highest lane, we will find God's vibration. We will find God. Once there, we've experienced God, then we can bring the experience back into this dimension when we come down.

So, we can say God is always here; It is an energy that is always here. We simply have to choose to allow ourselves to tune into Its frequency, and separate from the things that distract us from realizing It is *always* here.

Everybody has either the same or similar experiences. For example, this is one dimension. Does everybody in this dimension tend to experience the same thing? The answer is *yes*. Then, of course, the answer would also be *no*.

There are so many things to experience. There are some things we haven't experienced, yet. In each lane, or each doorway, we enter into what is already there. It's such a vast place; a person can spend significant time *experiencing*. So, it's more to say we have a desire to attain something.

Our desire may be to find relaxation, so we stay in the first level, or lane, to master it. We could decide we want to become more athletic and focus on our athletic skills to become better at what we do; therefore, we would stay in the first lane.

There is a part of us that says we need to know there is something more to life. We need to know there's something beyond these walls, this couch, and the way we understand reality and physics. Yet, we haven't experienced it.

Once we have mastered the first level, it's like somebody hands us a set of keys. This key is knowing how to hold our tonal. It's like holding our breath so we can move underwater.

We learn to maintain ourselves or steady our minds so we can move into this next dimension.

When we have entered this next dimension, we more than likely would find in that place something profoundly different than what is in this reality. The question is answered for us, now; it is acknowledged. We say to that part of ourselves, very deep within us, our Navigator: *It is true. There is something beyond all of this. There is something more.*

All we ever wanted was to stay in the second lane. We haven't even thought about a *third* lane. Maybe a person never will for the rest of their life. This is such a vast area a person can spend their entire existence going into this state of mind; remaining, exploring this particular frequency or dimension, and it becomes their ambition.

There are others who believe they need to experience God. They need to have some deeper fulfillment within life. Well, we have to master the first lane before the second, the second lane before the third, and so on, because it is in mastering these lanes that makes us able to move into other lanes. We cannot get in there, unless our consciousness has an understanding of what is expected from us.

You say God is everywhere, a dimensional frequency.
To experience other dimensions, we must shift our consciousness to higher frequencies, or lanes.
What is my frequency? Is it my energy? What determines my frequency and how do I change it?

Our thoughts, the things we experience in our lives, are what make our frequency. If we experience and reflect upon and do negative things, our tonal is never rich or high enough because all of these things are converted into our frequencies. Our energy vibration.

Everything we smell, hear, and taste is turned into electricity. Everything about our physical bodies is designed to convert this dimension into a format we can absorb because what are we? We are energy beings, more or less.

We are energy beings that exist within physical bodies made of living organisms. Not one part of what we think physically is ourselves, is truly who we are. It is other living organisms symbiotically working with us.

We are simply the energy they are speaking to, saying, "Okay, we're going to work with you. We're going to more or less do what you want."

Not everything we want comes from us. Half of what we want is the will of all these millions of organisms and a brain, which has its own personalities also. The reality is finding out who we are inside of all of this. Most people never discover this. They remain automated; this is what I call *sleepers*.

Sleepers are people who simply function in life and do their job, their role. They live life. A person who is awakened, is someone who acknowledges this is not completely who they are. They look at their hands, open them and close them, realizing it's a machine. They realize inside are bones like sticks and on top of that is clay.

We can look at the muscles. The body has electrical nerves that stimulate the muscles to expand and retract. The expansion and retraction is only machinery, a device to explore this dimension.

If we were to remove ourselves from this organism, from all of this flesh and matter, what would we be? We would be *energy*. Would we have ears to hear sound in this dimension? No. Would we have nasal glands to smell in this dimension? No. Would we have eyes to see the structural detail of this dimension? No.

We don't have eye cones to process the lighting and shading that bounce into our retinas. So, we could not experience this dimension if it wasn't for this organism, which is designed to hold our electrical energy. By holding the electrical energy, it is here to transfer the information of this dimension into electrical data, which is what we are.

It is like little raindrops in a bucket. Everything we smell, hear, taste, and feel is converted for us as electrical beings to add to what we are. Like a tuner to a channel, a radio station's specific signal, we are doing a watermark on the kind of being we are. The more we understand determines what kind of frequency we begin to radiate, allowing us to have access to moving into these other lanes.

The more we can conceive, the more we realize what we are; the more we reflect that there is more to life than what we see on the surface through our five senses. Then we begin to develop a *sixth* sense because it is a sense of knowing. This sense of knowing harnesses other ways of understanding life beyond this dimension. So, our frequency is based upon what it is we can comprehend and understand.

The effect of my previous conversation with you, alone, is what I call *shifting*. Our minds, energy-wise, are now reflecting more on what it is and is not. The more we reflect on what we *are*, the more we become that. The more we become that, the more conscious we are of what we *really* are, thus reality around us begins to change.

As we move into the first doorway, which is closest to the frequency of this world, we could say each lane, in and of itself, has micro-levels to it. We could say there are one hundred lanes inside one big lane we are working to move across. So, we are at the lowest portion of this lane.

Before we begin to move across this inner-lane, we go through change. The physical change happens in the lowest of levels. As soon as we begin to move into that, what happens is our bodies begin to re-adjust.

When we really think about it, in many cases our minds control how we physically feel in the first lane. Our muscles are directly related to our minds, which are electrical. As our hands expand and close, it is our minds that tell them to open and close. It is our will.

When we have tension or issues on our mind that are bothersome, without realizing it, our muscles tighten around our stomachs and hearts per se. They tense around other organs, which feel this tenseness to react. It misconstrues the natural cycle of information they are getting to function, as if there is a disturbance in the inner-universe, the micro-universe within us.

We are the God-consciousness of this extremely vast micro-universe within our body. All of these living organisms have some kind of lower intelligence, but they all are affected by *our* will.

When we are upset, it's like a force of energy as seen in the movie *Star Wars* known as *The Force*. It is affecting this micro-verse and not functioning well under a level that is peaceful or healthy for it.

When we meditate, it releases the tension in our bodies. When the tension releases from our bodies, our physical bodies begin to revert back to their normal process they know they should be in. Like resetting a flawed computer, it resets everything to the correct calibrations.

In a sense, by our first levels of meditation and taking that act, we're teaching our bodies to clear all these tensions out of it, allowing everything to relax or chill out. For example, organs in our throat may be secreting too many chemicals, thereby, creating anxiety or illness in us, or the effect of chemical pollutants because our bodies have created various chemicals. When it does this, everything gets a sense of what it needs to do, its job.

As we become more anxious and react in a flustered manner, we have to keep in mind the organs in our bodies are having the same reaction. So are all of the biochemical-producing glands in our bodies, creating an abundance beyond what they should. It creates a chain reaction within us, which leads to imbalance, whether it is psychological, physical, depression, health ailments, or telling ourselves to create cancer, tumors, or high blood pressure.

When we meditate, what we're doing is telling everybody, "Calm down. I'm going to take charge of my whole body for the first time, and we're all going to calm down and relax.

We're all going to get everything in order, so we all can be at peace within."

In the first lane, as we learn to master ourselves physically through meditation, we're learning to essentially talk to our bodies, that inner-universe. When this happens, we will notice simple things. For instance, after we finish meditating, we'll look younger.

This doesn't make any sense to most people, but it's really the truth. Our facial muscles reflect where our minds are at. If we have tension, our facial muscles become tense. People detect when there is certain tension within us.

When we meditate, these muscles relax. We don't need Botox to kill the nerves to relax the muscles in our faces. If we meditate, and the muscles naturally relax, it makes us appear younger and healthier. If we can imagine the external appearance of our faces then imagine what meditation does for us internally.

It relaxes our organs so they can function and produce biochemicals or whatever they need to do for our bodies. It affects the heart to beat at an appropriate rhythm for the whole inner-universe of our bodies instead of flushing and moving it too harshly, and so the liver and kidneys can do their job in such a way they are functioning properly. Our entire inner-universe is harmonized.

By harmonizing our inner-universe, we increase the quality of our health, the wellness of our being, and it allows our organs to begin the healing process, which they never had time to think about before because of the onslaught of mental electrical stimulation that was counterproductive to our inner-body balance. This is now being controlled by will because we are paying attention to what's going on.

Meditation is a choice. Most people never understand when we meditate, we have to sit down and make ourselves do it. Then when we're there, we find ourselves thinking: *my God, why don't I do this all the time?*

When we are living our everyday lives, and don't have a regular schedule to meditate, we forget about it and life takes over. It's another term for what we call *the DOE*. There is a vibration holding everything in place, telling every organism on the planet how to function. The planet is a living organism and that being has a specific vibration, not much different than how we have our own unique vibration. The difference is we live within this larger being and are constantly influenced by its energy. That's the DOE, a vibration, which is everywhere and affects all of us.

The proper meditation, which you will soon learn, serves to increase your own vibration. To raise you out of the DOE. To keep balance inside of our inner-universe. When we have learned to maintain balance, peace, and sanctuary, our frequency then has the ability, instead of being controlled, to begin to expand into higher levels of frequency. This is when we begin to move those microlevels to higher levels; those little lanes merge closer to crossing into the big lane.

At some point, we become skilled enough at controlling our emotions, the wellness of our being, how our minds operate, how we take in information, and how we clear our minds to view something. Again, some people would say, "Well, how does this all work when we study?"

Absent meditation, the mind races and starts to engage in excessive chitchat: *I've got to do this; I've got to do that; such and such is upset at me; I've got issues with this person and that person; I've got to find a job; I'm worried about money.* Meditation helps us learn to control chitchat; we are given a *system* to control it.

A big part is having the *system* to do it; this is what people don't have. They don't know how to do it, thinking: *How do I begin to have control? How do I take control?* So, you are going to learn how to take control.

When we have learned control, we can decide now is the time we have to sit down and study. We discipline ourselves to learn techniques to quiet the Babbler, or that part of us that's processing worrisome thoughts. It teaches us to remove things so we can simply focus our minds, and it seems very natural.

All of a sudden, the data we are reading comes to us not only clearer, but four, five, ten times faster. What previously took us four hours to finish now takes thirty minutes to complete. We absorb it all in full quality rather than needing to read it repeatedly.

Somehow we lost it. As in, we were reading, but it wasn't seeping in. Now, we know how to quiet our minds so we can fully absorb information.

Now, we need to look at the residual benefits. What previously took us four hours to complete, now takes about a half hour, which allows three and a half hours more to dedicate to something else. Not only this, but the quality of our lives improves because now we can master what it provides for us financially. We're able to achieve the goals we set more efficiently, with less stress.

It's self-purifying because the money gained from achieving our goals due to our study—giving us opportunities, perhaps, to earn more money, or whatever our goal may be—now releases burdens, which worried us in the first place. Then we learn to simmer down so we can focus on things: monetary issues, paying bills, evaluating and re-evaluating the need for medications, addressing certain anxieties, etcetera.

Money in this dimension is a big factor. This is not to say it should rule our lives; it shouldn't. The idea is to escape it so we can achieve it. Remember, escape it to achieve it. This is a very powerful statement to reflect upon. In order to do something, we have to understand its meaning; otherwise, it is pointless to do what we don't understand.

In this day and age, everybody wants immediate satisfaction. It is the McDonald's era of instant gratification; often people don't even think about what they are eating. It's like chomp, swallow, move on.

The point is, if we continue to live with this mentality, we're going to begin and end our lives without even knowing we existed. At the end of our lives, perhaps, we will become wise enough to know we need to reflect on things. However, by that time, our lives are already over, it's too late.

Learning to meditate and comprehend, we must have an understanding of what we're trying to do during meditation. This is the only way we are going to find the higher frequencies we yearn for.

Most people who spend twenty years meditating, never sit down to achieve anything but how to relax themselves. They fail to find those other doorways or experience anything else. It is not due to a lack of curiosity; it's not because they don't want to do so. It's because they never had a foundation to help them understand what they are seeking.

We could be sent on a mission to go to a certain place, but if we aren't instructed about what we need to achieve, how will we achieve it? The only people who achieve it, are the people who accidentally stumble across it.

Well, if you want to put all of that to chance, that is your business. I would rather stack as much in my favor as I can, which brings us back to this very discussion. This conversation is the very information to get you what you want.

You may say, "Well, I understand that already." *You* understand already, but there are people who don't. As much as they don't understand something and you do, rest assured as this discussion continues, there will be much you didn't realize either.

Afterwards you may say, "Now, I understand. I get it."

The only reason you never got it before is because you had the same attitude you have now: "I already understand all of that." No. As a teacher, trust me, you don't understand because if you did, you would be where I am at.

Anybody can achieve it. Meditation is a choice. The only way we will not achieve it is if we simply do not apply ourselves. If we don't sit down and declare we're going to do this, or we don't listen to what is being discussed, we assume we know it all. We will not be able to achieve it because we have already limited ourselves with assumptions. We have brought ourselves back down into what I call *the DOE*.

The DOE is likened to the central energy for the whole planet. It tells everything what it needs to be and its function.

The planet is a living organism and the human race is the central nervous system of the planet.

All species of life serve as some greater or lower protozoan organism of life. Meaning, we have red and white cells, and other living organisms in our bodies.

On earth, lions are a form of organisms, their own species. Schools of dolphins are a species to themselves, and the same with elephants, etcetera. Human beings are the highest level of inhabitant organisms, but we all work together. The human mind uses electricity for thought. So, every living creature—whether it is a plant, tree, or insect—has a frequency of electricity.

Now, if we look up the word electricity in the *Encyclopedia Britannica*, we will find numerous references about neurons, protons, photons, electrons, and so on. The truth of the matter is, we don't know what electricity really is. Understanding this, each species has a certain kind of frequency that's attuned to its species only.

For example, in our bodies, our liver understands what it needs to do for the rest of the body. In itself, the liver is made of millions of living cells specific to the liver only. They are not the same as heart or kidney cells. However, in some ways, liver cells are more advanced than maybe kidney cells, but in other ways, heart cells are more advanced than liver cells.

Cells are similar to a micro-universe, but in the end they all work together to create one thing, one giant being. So, one plus one in this case equals one, in a very chaotic way of thinking.

The planet has species that act as organisms, independent, yet in unison. We all work and live together. In some ways, we are dependent upon one another to exist, whether it be as plant life and vegetation, or meat eaters or carnivores. Certain carnivore creatures eat other carnivores, which is an inner-micro-system representing the living thing.

The planet cannot be viewed as a human being with legs and arms; it is alien. Meaning, it is extremely different from what we perceive. The point is, if we look at the cells of our bodies surrounded by organisms floating around, it's rhythmic: one-two, one-two, one-two.

One represents everything: *circular organisms.* Two, the next level higher, represents objects standing on four legs with arms and hands. Then, again, back to one, on a larger level. We would see the planet resembles the first one; like an organism, but different.

So it's alien, but this does not mean it's not alive; doesn't have its own organisms to work it; or doesn't know how its nervous system functions. It's just different, simply perspective.

If we stepped out of the planet and looked down at it, it becomes a spherical body floating in space. We should not see boats, cars, trees, houses, or who is playing baseball. We'd see one thing. Then if we zoomed in on it—we would see the micro world and all its complexities.

We collectively have a planet that has an agenda. Much like our bodies, it tells all of the organisms in it their roles. Although they are independent, there is constantly a vibration from us that tells them their place.

If everything acted outside of its function, there would be chaos. Life would diminish and be destroyed on the planet. However, because there is a vibration holding everything in a certain format of how things are to be and need to work, it keeps everything in a certain place. That's the DOE, a vibration, which is everywhere and affects all of us.

When we meditate and do spiritual things, we are trying to move into another place beyond this realm of reality, this world in which we are biologically a part. But remember, who we are is not who we really think we are. We are not this biological person. As long as we think this is who we are, we will always be in the DOE because the biological part of us belongs in this frequency.

We are energy beings coexisting in a physical body. *This* is the part of us, if it has any awareness, which says there has got to be more to all of this. It is the part of us that wants to escape or move out of the DOE.

Through meditation, understanding, and reflection about these inner-energies, we empower our vibration to move into higher frequencies, which move out of the DOE vibration range. When we move out of the DOE vibration range, we begin to experience things beyond what we feel and sense in this dimension.

That is ideally our goal, to move beyond what is being forced on us as the conditions. We're trying to find a way to escape, yet still remain in it somehow; one foot out of the lane and one foot in water, more or less.

We want to have our cake and eat it, too. We want to feel something spiritually, something to move inside of us to which we feel drawn, which is moving towards these higher frequencies. However, by the same token we know that we are part of the earth and need to be here to do something.

You say be spiritual, but don't get stuck in the DOE.
You say we are trying to find a way to escape it,
yet still remain. Isn't it a contradiction
to get out, but stay in?

We are discussing an *extremely* complex concept, yet this book is intended to present it as simply as possible. Admittedly, the challenge lies in balancing intricacies known to readers, who easily comprehend this theory, yet also consider readers, who may find this information difficult to absorb.

There are different types of people. It's not to say we all belong to a uniform human race that has no differences. In our bodies we have red and white blood cells. It could be considered in some ways our blood, but these red cells are the greater majority. They work to serve our bodies—they bring oxygen and minerals, heal wounds.

White cells, which are more limited, fight as part of the immune system. They have the ability to recognize a virus in the body, size it up then deal with it. In many cases, the white cells exhibit interesting levels of intelligence. They literally acknowledge a virus then summon other white cells until there are enough of them to deal with the virus. This is a definitive form of intelligence.

The world will always have red cells. People who assist the world in continuing to function but lack the instinct, or sense, to tap into the consciousness behind it. There will always be people who do not understand what *we* are after. There are those of us who have what I call the *navigator*. It is an instinct to find what we are seeking; nothing seems right:

- How do you know that?
- Did you read all of the books about that religion? No.
- Did you master the philosophical understanding of that religion? No.
- How do you know? It's an instinct.

It's an inherent instinct whereby a baby knows to suckle milk from a breast, or a salmon knows to swim up the river to its spawning place. It is natural.

Human beings have an instinctive soul. This energy tells us we struggle to find our source of origin. For the most part, *we* are trying to do it. We are trying to awaken. However, many people will never do it because the DOE is too strong, like a current pushing against a salmon swimming upstream to return home.

Now, the river has dams created by humankind and are dried up due to weather patterns. There are other obstacles like bears catching salmon and circumstances of nature. Everything struggles to prevent the salmon from making it back to its place of origin. Only the few will do it. The DOE is the same for awakening Navigators.

There is no sense of doom that the whole planet is going to become white cells and destroy the entire ecosystem. Over time, the earth must adapt and change to a higher vibration of beings living on it. It is not ready to do it in one sudden leap.

It will change much like evolution changes organisms to adapt, and it is a better place. The world is striving to get there, but it is all about time scales and being able to perceive these time scales.

There is no fear of those of us who find it that is a problem. It is not finding it. If we don't find what we're looking for at this stage of the world's evolution, in itself this is the destruction we are concerned about. If we don't find it, the ecosystem also messes up.

We need people to reach a higher sense of consciousness and to bring knowledge from those states back to help the red cells reflect in smaller ways, perhaps so they can lift the world tonal, collectively.

We need also higher beings to achieve this so viruses— the negative things that come into the world, whether they be beings, entities, etcetera—are countered by white cells powerful enough to deal with them, or they will wreak havoc on the world as we understand it.

There must be a system of balance in order for life to advance. When this is not done, what happens when we don't have white cells in our bodies and have viruses enter them? Eventually, our lives are terminated.

There has to be a checkmate process as we proceed from A to Z, so the world has an agenda it is trying to achieve. The planet, as a living, evolving organism is trying to achieve something. We have to look at it in terms of millions of years, not in our lifetime. However, in our lifetime could be the effect that destroys anything in the future. Hence, a counter process is a necessity.

The question becomes: What kind of intelligence does the planet have?

Is it like us, having conversations with other planets in the galaxy? Like, "Hey, how is the weather on that side of the galaxy?"

The planet is so alien and such a unique kind of organism. For us to perceive it would be similar to the organisms in our bodies trying to perceive what they are a part of. It does not have the certain complexities we have, in the manner in which we have them. If we could be an existing intelligence, except with limited experiences outside of ourselves, we would be more humble, pure, and simple, yet capable of understanding more.

The earth has a sense of wanting to exist—life. This sense of life is going to be what we are looking at and what we are trying to help it achieve. Our bodies, and all living organisms, have a sense to live. They want to live.

We want to live, don't we? If we were having a threatening experience, like teetering on the edge of a bridge, would not our whole body rebel, the muscles tense up, and our breathing pick up?

There is a sense of *wanting* to live and have safety. The planet has this effect, wanting to exist because it wants to achieve something.

When the earth has arrived at the point where it has experienced all it needs to experience, perhaps in some way, it will create its own soul by the same method of reflection. Reflecting on its experiences creates enough electricity to generate an energy that goes beyond matter, the physical.

Its *flesh* would be the mountains, oceans, and lava from the earth's core, which is its heart. In itself it would achieve this electrical energy so when it dies, it will then be able to move into some other existence different than ours, which gets into a whole different kind of lane for it to move into versus our lanes, which would be a different type of lane in itself.

It's very complex teaching at this juncture, but we are simplifying things to understand the big picture.

***

Now, let's look at religion. Any path that promotes life, kindness, and love is good. People have to grasp what they can. Everyone is not ready for this teaching, or to understand what is trying to be conveyed.

We are a people on this planet, who are not in the thousands, but the millions. We are here searching. We know no religion on earth is the *right* religion, and hopefully what I have to say will be enough for people to find whatever it is they are seeking.

We must go back in time to look at the planet, nomadic man, the caveman or primitive man, or whatever we want to call them. We have to understand there is one interesting thing that came from this period. As time progressed, people began returning back to the people they came from.

Let's say we came from Africa as a race, or evolution-wise came from monkeys to become humans. This is an entirely different conversation in itself, but the point is we came from one people. We split up, went out into the world, and developed differently, yet we were very similar.

What is very interesting about all the cultures of the world is *every* culture had an instinctual sense of God, an instinctual sense there was something beyond them. They tried to then interpret what this was.

There was no manual to tell us specifically what it is, and because humans were evolving in intelligence that was beginning to grasp or be able to take in this concept, it was very simple, like a child trying to perceive religion.

What would happen is, humans had clans and they walked the earth. Within these clans, there more than likely was a structure because humans are a very structuralized species. They had designated jobs: hunter-gatherers, nurturers, leaders, warriors, and healers. Everybody had their usefulness.

If they didn't have usefulness during this time when it was very hard to survive, they were very likely let go because it was too hard to feed them. So, unless they could contribute something to the group, they were in a lot of trouble.

The shaman would be either the one wounded, had a bad leg, or had some kind of problems preventing him from being a hunter. Perhaps, later in life he became the shaman versus the hunter because in early life he was healthy.

This shaman, medicine man or spiritual leader for this group, usually had more time to sit and reflect. He wasn't as busy in the physical way of having to gather food, find shelter, stake out the territory, and scout it out for danger. Instead, he reflected.

They would find moments to sit and go into the meditative state of mind talked about. They did this more often than the others. This is when they began to reflect on deeper thoughts, or at least whatever they could.

This is one way they evolved. They formed a higher intelligence because they used a different kind of thinking than the others. It wasn't really a *higher* intelligence, but it was a different proficiency of thought within their brain. Hunting was a skill which required a specific intelligence in order to do it.

However, self-reflection developed the mind in a different way. Whatever part we use is like a muscle—it is what we exercise. So, the shamans were the ones who reflected.

What happened is the shamans would be walking and all of a sudden a lightning bolt would come from the sky and it hit a tree. The tree would be on fire and there was a big boom and a bang. A light flashed.

Everybody would be terrified. All of the primitive people would think: *Oh, my God! What are we going to do?*

They would scatter, panting hard, and their hearts would race. Who would they look to? They looked at the shaman because his job was to have an answer for everything they encountered. This is why they fed and sheltered him—they needed comfort.

Anything we don't understand—and this is a broad statement—we fear! This comes from primitive times and holds true to this day. Not that this is a bad thing, as it is what kept us alive. The point is: living in constant fear is the problem. So, these people would look at the shaman as if to say, "Well, what do you have to say?"

When human beings had this shaman, and he was forced in a situation to come up with an answer. All of these people were in chaos and fear. They were looking at him, expecting he's supposed to understand this. He's the great shaman. He's got great insight.

He then would probably make up a lie. He would make up an answer to comfort the people, who were watching this fire. So, the shaman—after seeing the lightning bolt, fire, chaos, and all people looking at him and knowing his job was to have an answer— would create an answer.

He would basically lie, saying, "This was the thunder gods, who made lightning, uh, to give us a gift. The gift is the fire, which will feed us and give us life. We should worship this life."

Now, the fear turns to, "Oh, it was scary, but it came from the gods. They are the ultimate power and now we have this fire."

We have to metamorphose this over thousands of years, and now what we have are the makings for religions, belief systems built upon the construct of previous ideas.

Then somebody would come along every hundred or thousand years, who would reinvent the wheel, more or less.

So, if we look historically at religions, whether Christian, Buddhism, or Hinduism, we will find they all evolved from some other belief system. As we follow this back, they metamorphosized from something else, until we get back to the most primal essences of fear and comfort as concepts.

What we have to think about is where this need came from? There was a need to interpret God. There was a need to interpret what we sensed as a vibration or a feeling there was something beyond all of us.

There was a presence of the Force, Prana, or energy—a presence of a consciousness—we sensed and wanted to comprehend in our limited ways. To get closer, or the hopes of getting closer, to what led to the idea of building concepts for us to approach this in a way we could relate, we make God the only thing we can relate to with our intelligence: *a man.*

God became a man and the servants of God were also doing something we couldn't: fly. From there we have angels, and so on.

We interpreted life in a grandiose way; it would ideally be something we wanted to move towards, but it's not so much the interpretation of it. It's the idea every civilization on the earth felt the need to find a way to draw closer to a Presence they felt, interpreted, and created a concept that worked for them.

When we meditate that's the hardest thing to deal with and will be the one thing we will always have to contend with: the *Babbler*. The Babbler is a voice in the back of our heads. As we try to meditate and have clarity in our minds, the idea is not to speak and have words vocalized in our thoughts.

An example of this is when we sit, meditate, and try to attain non-thought then all of a sudden, we think:

- *I better get that laundry done today because tomorrow I won't have time, and I need something to wear to work; or*
- *Boy, I better do my grocery shopping later.*

Suddenly, there's another part of our consciousness that rationalizes: h*ey, wait a minute, Shut up. I'm trying to meditate. This is not the time to babble.*

Then we're quiet, again.

One of the things we learn in meditation is to control what's going on upstairs in our minds. Most of the things we are affected by in life are things happening *to us*. Meaning, someone knocks on the door as we're relaxing then comes in with all sorts of problems—we feel this person's anxiety and get caught up in the drama.

At other times, we may have a mate say, "I don't know how we're going to pay for things. We're going to lose our house."

These are anxieties heaped on us that we have rattling through the echoes of our minds. We have all of these demands on us.

We're told to sit down; push aside all of our anxieties, problems, people bringing us issues who invade our worlds, or disturb us; and give ourselves enough mental attention to read a book we will be graded on. The goal is to read without our minds wandering or thinking other thoughts.

Then, we stop reading because we didn't grasp what we needed from the read passages. Now, we have a conscious, babbling thought: *I need to shut up.*

We refocus ourselves and try to absorb the information by reading it again. It may take three or four attempts to read one page until we actually gain something from it because we've been disturbed repeatedly by the thoughts, problems, and issues running through our minds.

With meditation, we learn a skill to quiet that part of the Babbler. This particular skill limits the amount of disturbances. The technique trains us to be effortlessly disciplined to eventually read one page without having to re-read it two or three times to understand what we need from it.

We're going to read it one time and comprehend it. We're literally going to flip the page, read it, internalize it. It's similar to reading something we really want to read that holds our attention versus reading something we are assigned, but really have no interest in.

We have to look at our minds. It's fascinating that when we're interested in something, we're disciplined, but when we're not interested, in most cases, it's very hard to hold our concentration.

Somehow, people who succeed in life naturally learn this skill; it's a form of meditation. It's a form of self-disciplining and using one of the skills we've practiced in our meditation to achieve a meditative state-of-mind. It's a skill we can use in other areas of our lives.

Similar to wax on, wax off as depicted in the movie *The Karate Kid*, the student learns skills he didn't realize he could use from a simple movement. It can accomplish more than one thing.

During meditation, we learn to calm ourselves and clear our heads while at the same time, learning to focus more easily on schoolwork, achieving a goal, or accomplishing what we want to do with our bodies, and so forth. This is how extremely useful meditation can be.

There are other schools of thought. One of the most interesting things is when we meditate we don't want to have thought. Yet, what most people fail to understand is when the spiritual teacher(s) say, "You want to have non-thought," they're not saying don't think. They're suggesting if we stop thinking, the effect is we'll think in a different way.

We won't have words in our heads, but we'll have thoughts. We won't have thoughts, but we'll be able to acknowledge movements of awareness, meaning we're thinking, but at a higher level. So, we stop the Babbler and can look across the room and acknowledge everything in the room. Someone can speak to us and if we want to respond, we can speak to them.

We don't have to think about what to say or how to react. We already know.

The idea is to learn during meditation to have a higher state of consciousness than the way we now think. By learning to have non-thought and teaching ourselves to not think with words or pictures, there is a different way of developing an intelligence with which we actually think. It's hard for us to perceive, but it's the truth.

An example would be for you to not think for five seconds. We're going to test the ability of your will to control your mind.

If you are with someone, ask them to stop their thoughts. If you ask this person not to speak aloud for two minutes, for sure they would feel confident enough to do it. If you ask the same person to quiet their mind and not speak in their mind or out loud, you would think the average person has this ability. The point of this test is to put the Babbler, talking within one's mind, to the test. If you were able to do five seconds, try thirty seconds and then one minute. See how long it takes your Babbler to rebel against your will. Then see if you can do the same amount of time by simply not speaking out loud. Why is controlling the mouth, not speaking, easier than controlling thoughts? Both should respond to our will, correct?

Part of it is practice. We have assumed mastery of the external world and neglected the internal. We learned as children to behave and gain control as adults of our actions. Yet, in our own thoughts, we remain as children where very little discipline has been exercised. The other part is that our thoughts are not completely us. It is a collection of the will and desires of the millions of organisms that make up our bodies, which manifests as the Babbler.

Here is another test. With a partner silently select about five objects near you. Don't let the other person know what you have randomly selected. It can be a pen, candle, cup, etcetra. Anything you have near you. Without saying a word, pick up each object, hold it up for about three seconds, and put it down then pick up the next object, show it, then put it back down. If you are alone, use the images in this book for the same purpose. Look at each image without saying what they are.

When you're finished, the other individual has to tell you what each object was you held. The trick is while you hold up each object, the person is to be silent during the process and experience non-thought. They cannot say in their mind what each object was, or use any other trick to occupy the mind other than silence.

This other participant shouldn't hum, sing any songs, or make any noises to cause distraction. This person should feel relaxed and non-verbally look at and identify each object. More than likely, this person is going to fail.

The other person will name at least one of the items, for sure. In most cases, they will name all objects. But did they maintain non-thought

Look at each object without saying what they are in your head.

while they did this? The point of this test is to demonstrate lack of inner-control. The following questions ultimately need to be examined: Who is in control? What is in control? It certainly isn't our will or desire not to speak. We really shouldn't have to be concerned about having this level of control in our minds. Why the struggle? That's the Babbler. It's a part of the organic brain (the machine) that believes it's reflecting us. It's imitating us; it's part of the DOE. It is so used to doing the program of the DOE that it automates us. This is what we call being in a sleep, going through life not really aware or conscious of what we're doing. This is the DOE—it's programming.

So, when we meditate, the first thing we learn to do is control the part of our minds that has unknowingly controlled us. We always thought we were in control; these are *our* thoughts. However, they're not our thoughts.

Now, we need to recognize something different. If we learned not to say what was in our thoughts, that other kind of intelligence already knew what all those objects were. It already knew what the pen and cellular telephone were; there was no need to say it aloud.

When we meditate, our goal is to achieve this type of intelligence without using words. When we perceive or think about something, if we could do it without words, how much faster would we be able to do it?

Instead of little cars of a train, each piece of the train is a word. *Today* is a word. *I'm* is a word. *Going* is a word. We have to say these words non-verbally, have these thoughts, or start analyzing with our thoughts. What if we could remove all that and simply be aware? We wouldn't need to use any of those slow, clunky words, yet acknowledge all of the information in our minds.

When we learn to do this, to sit down and read a book, we find we read faster. We absorb the information faster. When we try to achieve a goal athletically, we master it better at a higher performance. When we try to better our health, rather than having to focus on it, our awareness is so clear, sharp, and defined it just happens because we are willing.

Another term we'll use is: *intent*. Intent is a teaching word; what is our intention? If our intention is to feel better about our health, when we meditate, we need to have that conscious thought inside. It's about getting better and we'll get better.

What we're really doing is with intent, we know when we're meditating without any thought, the session is about becoming healthier and better. For some reason, cells and organisms in our bodies, *per se*, simply feel that presence better than when we use rudimentary words or have to think in such a construct way.

Meditation helps us to think clearer and faster; it helps us retain information better. Initially, it's something we have to learn to do and become used to it. This comes from practicing meditation. It's wax on, wax off.

We won't realize we're doing it. It's the by-product of, all of a sudden—something we realize we can do without realizing we ever could before. It just happens to us. The point is, where are our minds? Our minds are not thinking in words.

When I go into meditation, there're different avenues for what I am trying to achieve. On one level, I'm relaxing my body because what did I say earlier? The first thing we learn in meditation is to calm our bodies, so the stresses can be relaxed and to have clarity. In order for me to go to the higher levels where I go, like everyone else, I have to clear my physical body. I separate my mind from it, because as an organism, it's going to function perfectly on its own.

When a person goes into a coma, does the body instantly stop functioning? If the mind has ceased, in most cases, the body will still function. It's a living thing on its own. Most people's fear of meditation keeps them from achieving anything really advanced, because there's a fear of death.

This is one of the biggest things when we cross lanes. As we head into bigger lanes, one of the things we have to conquer is our fear of death. What's keeping us here, psychologically, in the back of our minds is the fear of not being able to return to our physical bodies because we believe still, with all of our training, it is who we are.

When we finally accept it's not completely who we are, we can leave it and become free. We can move into the higher lanes or into the presence of God because it's our realization. In spiritual terms, it's what realization is; this is what they mean.

When I meditate, the first thing I do is remove myself from my body. Now, my mind is moving into higher dimensions, or I'm moving very quickly. We don't move *through* those dimensions; we simply go *to* the dimension, or that frequency we choose to be.

There's no sense of linear movement; we go into frequency. Sometimes, I will do it solely to relax and I'll stay in that first lane because it's all I need to do. Other times, I will move into the third, tenth, or hundredth lane, depending on if there's information I need to acquire, or if I need to convey something important to this higher frequency, expecting a higher intelligence to return back to me with information.

For example, the planet is a living organism, and as such, it has a kind of intelligence. This intelligence is hard for us to perceive. It's very alien, but in simpler terms, it's to say people like Edgar Cayce and other spiritual groups of people from history or civilizations refer to there being a kind of collective library or the Akashic records. It is a place where we could find great knowledge.

However, when people hear those terms, they think it's a place we go. We drive our cars and it's a giant library, like the Library of Congress, or it's someplace they go as a spirit to see their spirit bodies walking down the hallway talking to the other spirit beings. This is not how it works.

The planet, Gaia, has a mind and its consciousness is a vibration. A spiritual person goes into the point where they can clear their mind and have an intent to understand, to know something; an intent void of words because words can't enter these places. It's too low of an energy.

It's not clear enough because when we're moving into higher frequencies, frequency is moving faster. We have to move at the same speed. So, we can't necessarily be in our lane and have a car that has a 4-cylinder pulling a tractor behind us if we're going in the 90 MPH lane, right?

It's like we've got to leave it behind temporarily then come back for it later. We've got to leave our bodies and all their lower sensory behind, so we can move our energy beings, the part of us that's electricity, to those higher frequencies and get what it needs and come back.

When we enter this state, we can go to the Gaia frequency, which would be the Akashic records, or the library. It's the mind of Gaia and we simply have an intent of needing to know, or understand something; we simply know it or in a certain way, comprehend it.

We have an epiphany all of a sudden, like we had an old memory resurface.

We say, "Oh yeah. How did I ever forget that?"

Suddenly, we understand it. It's not like we sit and it's being read to us in any kind of format that we're used to in this dimension. We don't have to look it up; we simply need to know it and it's revealed to us.

It was always in our minds. In some cases, when there are things I need to know regarding the world, people, individuals, etcetera, there are times I will go to this Gaia mind and simply know what it is I need to know.

We, as living organisms, have a recorded memory of everything we've ever done since the moment of our birth. The machinery of our bodies has been recording sound, smell, sight, hearing, and taste since the moment of our conception.

Therefore, all data is recorded. Whether or not we, as the main consciousness, can extract it at will remains to be seen, but we may with practice. We don't exercise that part, so it's not flexible enough to go there, yet.

Gaia, or the planet, remembers everything. It's also being recorded. By going to that mind or place, we can gain knowledge. In our bodies, we could say white cells fight a cold and we never catch the same cold twice because it learns the virus; it has a library of information.

It goes to a kind of consciousness we're not even using with all of this data. It has a memory of its own. It says, "Okay, here's the virus. We need to remember how we destroyed it before."

In a micro-sense, we are that God-consciousness for our bodies, as the planet is for us, as the universe is for everything. It finds that information and brings it or we bring it back, or the organisms in our bodies can use it for a database to know how to deal with things.

So, when we are asked what's going on in our minds, our minds are not using thought. Our minds are getting information to help the world.

My experience is either to relax myself or get away from it all by taking a mini vacation. I also meet with other beings. If we should go in this direction, they convey what's going on with them and we counsel one another as to how to deal with certain circumstances or things that are happening in other dimensions or realities. We do this in order to help something much bigger than everything most people can understand.

The question is: how does meditation help the planet as an organism, since we are micro-organisms, who are part of this collective consciousness? We have what I call *nodes* (neural synapses) in the brain, of which we have billions or trillions. If we have one node stimulating a balance for the whole consciousness, there are balancing and chaotic factors in our consciousness all the time.

Our immune system is being challenged every second. Our psychological state is being challenged every moment because we have many things going on in our lives. We may have to go to work and deal with something we may not want to deal with. We may have to deal with family issues, problems, or health issues.

There are parts of our mind constantly trying to keep us in balance. These parts would be for the planet, what we are (as meditation people) doing for ourselves.

In retrospect, we are already contributing to the balance of the planet. What we want to do is create greater balance, a more proliferated amount of balance, for the world. In so doing, the world then can accelerate to a higher state of consciousness because there's a greater amount of balance for the majority of its existence. The planet can then achieve higher states.

As an energy being inside of a physical body, the body interprets the senses into electricity for us as an energy being. So, the body's an all-terrain vehicle (ATV), a physical machine that interprets electricity.

A lot of times I will ask students to imagine a television and its apparatus, or its purpose is to capture what we cannot experience. All of the radio signals and data—millions of channels of sound and pictures, and information and explanations—are untouchable within our physical body.

This apparition, this square box, will capture information and transfuse it, then bring it out into the open in a format we can experience. So, the physical body transforms this dimension in the opposite way. It turns this dimension into electrical energy for us to experience as energy beings inside of our physical bodies.

Which begs the question: when we as energy beings leave our physical bodies, how is it we interpret what we experience? Obviously, we don't have the same five senses we would have if we were simply energy. So, what are the senses of an energy being?

A scene in the movie *The Matrix*, they say the matrix cannot be explained, it has to be experienced. Well, imagine the opposite—we are trying to perceive something that goes beyond anything we can remember in our physical existence to help us interpret it.

The human brain uses interpretation for it to grasp things. In other words, we look at other things we've experienced to bridge concepts, so we can understand something else. We have to understand sociological thinking.

When we leave our bodies and are energy beings, since we think we are still human beings, we limit our perception. For instance, most people who have an out-of-body experience will see things as if they see it with their normal sight.

We can't see behind us because we don't have eyes behind us. We can't see out the sides of our heads because we don't have eyes on the sides of our heads. We have a certain spectrum of vision. Since it doesn't occur to us as energy beings that we should be able to have three hundred and sixty degree vision, a full spectrum of vision, we limit our perspective.

Therefore, we will find much of our experiences will be very similar; not exact, but similar to when we are in a physical body. We will only be able to interpret as much as we're willing to accept to understand. The brain has a certain system of interpretation.

For example, take your middle finger of whichever hand you use the most and your index finger then cross them. Begin touching your nose when I instruct you to do so. Your brain is wired to interpret your nose as one nose. What's going to happen as you start to touch your nose with your two fingers crisscrossed is your brain is going to interpret you have two nose tips.

Go ahead and do it. You'll experience a different kind of sensation. It's as if your nose is not completely the way it should be; the more you touch it, the more your brain going to create that second nose. It's not just going to stop; it's going to perceive a second nose.

Do you have two noses?
How much can you rely on the brain
alone to interpret reality?

Here's another example. If you have a pen in your hand, take the pen and close your eyes. Take the pen and run it over those two crossed fingers. Your brain will sense there are two pens, but you must close your eyes.

Now, when you open your eyes and look at what you are doing, your sight is a greater sensory than your finger. So, looking at the pen run over your two crossed fingers will correct the information so you only feel one pen. Having demonstrated this, the same thing goes for when we leave our bodies.

Take the pen and drop it in the V-space between the two fingers. Spread them as far apart as you can then guide it back and forth with your eyes closed. Feel the touch.

Don't simply run it up and down; go from left in the valley then out to the other side. Go over the humps and see how it confuses you. If you open your eyes and look at it, it will adjust to the correct way the eye should interpret this activity.

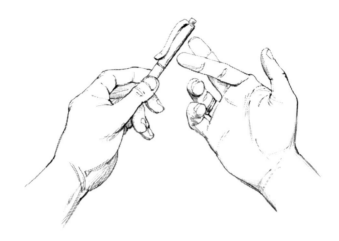

Are there two pens?
Our perception is limited by the senses we use.

So, how we view life is interpreted by the brain in a very unique way also. Understanding this, we've learned something new. When we leave the body, we will perceive things in the way we expect to perceive them until it dawns on us that we should be able to perceive differently. It's almost the opposite, so we will begin to see in a three-hundred and sixty degree perception.

We will have a different sense of hearing, taste, everything because it's not normal sensory. Also, we will discover senses we have no words to describe. What we experience will take time to accept; the more we operate with a higher way of thinking, without words, the faster we will gain these experiences.

As long as we think using words in our minds, we will never really be able to enter the second lane. We can't go there because the brain won't let us. We are still using our brains to interpret and comprehend with; it's designed to only comprehend this dimension. It's profound if you think about it. There's really an answer here.

Our brains really think in three formats. The first format is biochemically. When we have a thought, it spews out chemicals, which hit other chemicals to create an electrical storm. This storm creates, in a sense, data by creating that same pattern. By creating this pattern, it creates intelligence. It's how we store information.

If we have somebody around us, the more we see them the more our brains create a pattern of the person's face. When this person is not around as often as they were, the brain searches for that person's face pattern. When it doesn't see the face, it starts to release chemicals in the brain that create depression. It's similar to trying to find that face so it can be restored into our being.

This comes from childhood. Being a child and acknowledging our mothers or the same way an animal may represent its familiar area. The brain will secrete chemicals to create a sense of urgency to seek it out because it's not getting a static pattern of biochemical charges in the brain anymore. The pattern has changed, so it's trying to find the pattern to fit it. It's a very crude way of having intelligence, but it works.

The second format is what I call *low radiation impulse*, which is how the brain tells the body to breathe without verbalizing, "I need to breathe;" it tells us how to have our hearts pump, or our kidneys and livers to work. It's constant; the brain is telling it what to do.

Remove the brain then everything doesn't know what to do because it doesn't know how to work. It needs to be coerced and taught how to function as a whole system. Low radiation impulse is another way we think.

The third format is electrical, which is streams of electricity that shoot over to another synapses to actually create that chemical discharge with the organic. It can move thought.

Looking at it in a different way is: what most people are doing everyday of their life, what part of the brain they are using, is the first format: it's organic. Everything we do is biochemicals going off in our brains.

We have to do this; we have to do that. We're following these patterns created in our brains and feeling anxiety because of a need to fulfill them. This is how most people think; they are asleep. They operate using patterns running in their heads.

There are so many patterns; it seems like there's an intelligence transmitting. We're performing activities using these patterns all rather quickly.

The second format, low radiation impulse, is faster. It's the middle lane verses the slower lane, which is organic, biochemical thinking. So, the low radiation impulse moves at the speed of electricity, but not quite. This would be what we call a psychic state of mind, or using our sensory.

We're feeling what a house feels like if there's something in that house. We're using it to use our telepathic ability, if we are going to feel something from another human being. What we call the psychic realm or abilities stems from a middle way of thinking, that low radiation impulse. It's where we get psychic abilities.

These psychic abilities allow us to push the gateways of time and reality a bit, and physics as we understand it. However, it's not fully where we want to or could be. It's somewhat in-between.

The third format, electrical, is pure electricity, pure light. This is when we think without thought. The electricity follows brain tunnels, the organic brain, like train tracks. It remains on course, which is limiting because the brain communicates if we go off the tracks, everything will be chaotic. This is not necessarily truth.

When we can stop thinking with the organic and low radiation impulse brain, we purely enter the third format. This is when we shut out the Babbler because the Babbler is organic. It's the organic brain. It's too slow, heavy, and methodic. It's like being a horse-and-buggy on a ninety mile per hour road.

The next format is not a horse-and-buggy; it's like a 1940 Volkswagen Beetle. It's better than a buggy, but it sure isn't as good as using a Lear jet. The Lear jet is when we begin to think and perceive without that bulky method of thinking in our brains—using words, the Babbler, and everything else.

We train ourselves to think or perceive in pure light, which means we can move into higher frequencies and understand higher dimensions, higher possibilities. Our minds can move at this frequency so quickly, everything slows down to a level that seems understandable.

Like moving into that ninety mile per hour lane, in one sense, we're moving extremely fast, but in another, if we look at the car next to us, it seems as if we're not moving at all. By slowing ourselves down, we move faster.

Not only do we need to slow down, but we also need to let go. We need to surrender. Students often explain they sit down to meditate and willfully push so hard for something to happen that nothing at all happens. When they finally realize all they need to do is to sit back, relax, and surrender to allow whatever's going to happen to happen, that's when they have the best experiences.

This is why in meditation, we should *want for nothing*. Don't want for money, health, or anything. Our intent is already known—we already know we want to feel better, or find some higher meaning to our lives. We don't need to make it an organic constant in our minds. As long as we use an organic level of thinking, we remain in the twenty mile per hour lane.

By not thinking about it at all, intent becomes pure light. It doesn't have a weighty way of thinking, simply a sense of knowing where we need to be. We already know what we need to do. By trying to acknowledge this *wanting for nothing*, we are free to move from low radiation impulse thinking, to the electrical, staying in pure light.

The second the organic mind pushes a thought, which is the Babbler, it slows the light. It traps it and has to jump from hyper-speed into a lower speed. Suddenly, we're going from a high pitched tone to a low pitched tone, again. Now, we must untie and free ourselves until we escape again to move up into a higher frequency of consciousness. This is what is meant by moving slower to go faster.

What we think is our worst enemy, may be our greatest freedom. The most interesting part is the DOE—the twenty mile per hour lane, which is organic thinking—is a constant vibration. Similar to the scale of musical pitches: *Do-Re-Mi-Fa-So-La-Ti-Do.* The frequency we want to reach is: *So.* It's like pure energy, release, and non-containment of the lower dimension. It's really free; that's what we're looking for.

The DOE holds us down so we can't escape our physical bodies. The DOE has a very unique process: as long as we stay in it, we forget about higher frequencies. It almost erases our memory.

It's like when we have a fantastic dream. We're very excited about the dream when we wake up. Within moments, however, what happens to our memory of the dream? It begins to fade. In the dream we're somehow entering those higher lanes because we're not using our Babbler to think.

It's as if we've escaped our organic minds for a temporary moment to experience profound things. Our brain is trying to interpret these profound things. When we come out of it and are fully in this conscious reality trying to interpret it, everything slows down and vaporizes; it fades away. We lose that dream; we forget what it was all about.

The idea is we want to exercise our meditations. We want to exercise these thoughts, this kind of thinking. We want to gather with other people to have these conversations because it exercises a higher state of our awareness. It doesn't allow the DOE to lull us into a sleep.

If we're constantly exercising something then what do we learn in the physics of this world? We maintain the strength of it in most cases. When we don't exercise something, it fades away. So, staying awake means we know there's something beyond all this. We've experienced it.

Rather than go back into the DOE to throw away our methodic processes of life and every so often, like waking out of a dream for a moment, thinking we're awake in our dream for a moment only to realize we're still in a dream and we fall back into the dream. We don't remember we woke out of it two seconds ago.

We always have to, in a sense, fight to stay awake. The more we meditate, the more we practice these kinds of teachings, The more we maintain a higher consciousness it allows us to keep one foot in the realm of possibilities where we feel complete, wholesome.

It is a place where we find a balance between this reality and dealing with life, serving and helping the world and humankind, but in another place. We find the solitude, peacefulness, and completeness of what we're looking for, so the balance is *Higher Balance*; being in two different places at once, being a third, and being in the middle.

When we talk about all these other personalities inside us, the organic brain starts telling us, "You need to do this; you need to do that." We always thought it was us.

Well, the part that's really us, I call the *Middle Pillar*. We can't find ourselves until we've removed all the trappings we think are us, which gets into another conversation called *self-observation*.

Everything we've talked about goes back to meditation. Now, when we discuss meditation, we have a better idea of what is expected of us, where it is we're headed, and if we have an idea of where we're headed, we can relieve ourselves of anxiety, which again is organic fear that's keeping us in the lowest levels.

When we don't have a fear of where we're headed, we can get there a lot easier. This is the reason for "Foundation." Which goes back to realizing without understanding what we're discussing, we're never going to get where we want to go.

We have to perceive all this. We have to discuss them because it allows us to untie all the little knots holding our energy in our physical bodies. We have to embrace it's okay to move a little bit beyond this, expand our vibration. We're loosening all these knots holding us there.

When speaking about a fear of death, we, generally, are so afraid to die. We linger to a point where we can't even open the door to look outside.

What if something bad happens to us in life and we are mugged one day? So, now we stay indoors and lock the doors. We make everybody else do the shopping and bring it back, or go outside and tell us what happened. Our lives are spent in the house.

Can anybody say this is a good way to live on the planet? Of course not, but our fears hold us hostage, so our reality becomes the house. What we see on television or hear on the radio is our only link to the outside world.

The people who visit become our only link. They become our fingertips to the world. Our hearts desperately yearn to know what's going on outside, but our fears keep us inside our home.

Fear of death is like dying because we want to explore the other possibilities of what we are. The other possibilities of moving beyond what we understand or who we think we are to the concept of leaving our bodies can take on many concepts.

However, because we have an innate fear of death, we assume leaving our bodies will cause us to die when the truth is more than likely we never will. If we actually gained the courage to leave the house a few times, we may find we're more gratified by what's outside of life than what we ever perceived it to be.

In some cases, we don't even know we're afraid to leave. We've gotten so used to being in the house it never dawns on us we really want to leave; every part of us is wondering what's going on out there. This is why we cling to the television and people who come to visit. They tell us what they're doing outside of the house. We have to realize first, it's something we may want very much; somehow it helps complete us.

Everything in the house is familiar; you've probably touched, heard, seen, or smelled it a hundred times. There's nothing new stimulating our existence. There is nothing that makes us feel more complete. The only thing we hang onto is our existence of safety.

Some people may ask what the point is if everything we have to experience, we've experienced a hundred times. It becomes so mundane; there's nothing to stimulate our will to exist. Everything we are living for becomes what is brought in from the outside world.

It's what we itch for because it's something new; it's stimulation. It's some new thought. It's some person visiting with some new object they have brought along.

It's about realizing, self-realization. What we really need to do is venture out, realizing there's nothing outside that's going to harm us. We have to become fearless. In so doing, we will find our greatest strengths to conquer everything of which we're afraid.

We will find our fear could never conquer us to begin with. It could never kill, destroy, or control us. It could only do so because we accepted what it could do to us.

When we discuss death, everybody's in their body. Everybody wants to feel God. Everybody wants to feel a higher sense of something. Everybody wants a great adventure in life. Everybody wants to experience another world, reality, being, or something; they just want to know that as much as there's something ugly and evil possibly out there keeping them inside, there must be something opposite that is profoundly beautiful.

Life is wonderful—live life! It's worth living. There are other parts of us that want something more. We have to be willing to go outside to smell the roses and walk barefoot through water. Why should we fear leaving our physical bodies? It's simply moving through other ways and gaining other senses.

If we could never smell in our whole lives, would we say the reality of us experiencing scent was real or not real? It wouldn't exist. The moment we could smell, would we say we let ourselves smell? Would we say some part of us became better able to experience what always was?

So, experiencing dimensions is nothing to fear;
they are already here.
Like smells, they surround us. I simply lack
the sense, the sixth sense, to see them.

All these other dimensions are really one thing: they're all here at the same time. We find the other senses inside ourselves to activate them, so we can experience and help them reflect on us to become more of a greater being.

When we have more experiences in life, do they not make us more complex? Do they not gratify places the dubious areas within ourselves, where we built up strengths?

Because we've experienced, through our senses and putting ourselves in circumstances that expanded us, we develop spiritually, or our energy spiritually. We are then able to experience things much more profound.

If we could never smell before, all of a sudden the activation of this simple sensory would open up a vast door we never thought comprehensible. Imagine if we were deaf our entire lives—we learned to touch, taste, and see, which are very profound—yet, we never registered hearing. People have tried to explain it, but we couldn't relate because it didn't seem to matter.

Suddenly, we had the ability to hear one day. Our ears were filled. What would that do to us? We'd be in shock, speechless. Then all of a sudden, not only could we hear conversations, but when we thought it couldn't get any better, we venture into nature and start to hear birds and children laughing, another level.

Then, without warning, we enter another level of sound where we start to hear the wind blow through trees and the roar of ocean waves crashing into the shore. Then we begin to feel things inside we never felt before and hear sounds of music; music created by eyes and hands; music stretched and chords building, beckoning something deep inside primes us to burst open with joy.

This is what awaits us, but we have no idea it's been there the whole time. If we don't know it's there, it never dawns on us to look for it until somebody tries to let us know.

Somebody may say, "Hey, there's something I can show you. I know you're deaf, but I think we may be able to fix that for you."

That's what this is all about. Everybody's asleep in the world. Awaken and be amazed by what you find. Don't live life never knowing; be curious. Be cautious, but curious. We'll find what's inside each of us can be satisfied. The answers aching inside of all of us, without a name, can be enriched, healed, and completed.

To those of us who can hear, a deaf person may say, "There's something inside of me I'm yearning for. I don't know what it is, but you all seem to be a little happier than me. So what's up with that?"

If we could hear music all of a sudden one day, how much would it heal all of those empty places inside? Maybe not all of them, but many. This is meditation. On our path of life, somewhere we have discovered there's something more—we're on its track.

If we were deaf and instantly heard a booming sound, the experience may result in a heart attack. It would be so overwhelming.

If you had the heart attack, would you be afraid to die? Would you be in such awe your heart attack was an actual burst of amazement it set you free, somehow, to something beyond all this?

You're looking to go beyond—we all are. There's nothing wrong with it, and to settle for less we've simply chosen to be a red cell. We just want to exist, never wanting to reach beyond what we could perceive, or what we thought may have been. Maybe we can't perceive it, but the idea is to somehow poke around.

When we meditate, there's a phrase called *surrender*. Everybody thinks they understand the concept of surrendering.

Surrender means to stop worrying about everything, letting everything go, setting ourselves free.

As we meditate, we let it all go. We'll find the Babbler has no strength if we can just let it all go. What holds us to our five senses? What holds us to this reality is our need to stay here, our need to cling to things.

This discussion segues into another concept called *mindfulness.* Mindfulness is to be mindful of the predicaments we put on ourselves.

For instance, if we take a job, we need to be mindful of whether or not it is more work than we want to do. Will the job set higher demands on our lives, taking away personal freedoms? Are we willing to accept this?

If we let somebody move into our house to help them out, are we doing it because we need to help them, or are we being compassionate? Will having a person in the house, interfere with the solitude we need to keep the peace in our lives? Is one greater good better than another?

We need to be mindful of the decisions we make. They are going to affect us. Mindfulness is being aware of what we're putting ourselves into.

Mindful is the opposite of being *mindless* as we throw ourselves into things. We must not make quick decisions. Mindful means what holds us to this world, binds us from becoming a higher frequency, is going to be weighed by our brains.

Our brains are going to be connected to our minds; they are two different things. The brain is the organic machine; it's the Babbler. It's all these thoughts, pressures, and anxieties. The mind is the soul. It's what's trying to escape it all, thinking: *there's got to be something beyond all this.* The brain, however, almost hangs onto it, keeps it, and traps it.

The mind is constantly trying to free itself because it's the pillar. It's the *Middle Pillar.* So, mindfulness means to be mindful as conveyed in *Star Wars* when Obi-Wan, a Jedi master, tells his student, "Be mindful of The Force."

If we think about our spirituality a lot, this is where our spirit will reside. If we think about business all the time, it is where our spirit will reside. If we think about our problems all the time, it's where our spirit will reside. If we're mindful of the Force, it will reflect us. If we're mindful of our problems, our problems will be what we are; constantly in chaos, a wreck.

Being mindful of life will fill us with life. Therefore, mindfulness means thinking about what we're thinking! Think about what we're doing every day of our lives without thinking about it. Think about the decisions we're making and doing things without reflecting on who we really are, or giving it a moment of recognition.

Maybe you're not thinking of meditating, but if you did, and made yourself actually do it, in the process of starting, you think: *God, I'm glad I did this.* That's the DOE; that's the machine.

It's about trying to be awake and not let the DOE run us so much we've forgotten to stop and smell the roses. We need to stop and experience the beauty in life instead of letting life run us and its machinery, instead of being constantly in the DOE.

When we meditate, it's like saying:

- "I'm going to hug myself."
- "I'm going to reflect on the *Middle Pillar*."
- "I'm going to give a part of my life, moment, and day to be mindful of the Force."

We have made a decision because the energy of the DOE doesn't want us to go there. It wants us to be a red cell and to do our everyday thing. It wants to mull over any concept of escaping to any other place; that's all. We're there to serve it. It's like the red cells of our bodies; they are there to serve us.

Of course, we are much more complex and are part of the Universe. We are, in some ways, different than other people. Although we look the same, we are different. The more that we can understand this concept, the more it seems logical, and the more our vibrations move toward that higher frequency.

Remember, intelligence and recognition are living things. They are a vibration and if we exist *and* choose to exist there more often, it becomes who we are.

Chapter 3

Multi-Dimensional Meditation

We have a red and a blue energy. The blue is positive, red is negative. What we want to do is attract the blue. As we attract the blue, this is the fuel we need to collect into a reservoir within our bodies, our beings.

When we've collected enough of this energy we can then dispense it in different ways, whether it be to heal, enhance our minds, enhance our vibrations, our health, or our well-being. Whatever we want to use it for, this energy is something we need in order to transform it into a result or an effect.

Many people who are spiritualists are able to do things spiritually or attain certain states of mind, advise they can only do these things or attain states to a certain point then they've exhausted their energy. This is because they don't understand the principle of absorbing Prana. That is, absorbing this energy in so they can collect it and use it to build their energy fields, to build the essence and vibration of themselves in order to do things spiritually.

Even more so, our energy needs to hit a certain frequency to move into other places. In another way, we can say we need to fuel this energy to move into other frequencies. This is the fuel we're absorbing to enhance our vibration and tonal then we're going to set a certain pitch to it by our consciousness.

We need this energy to come into us so we can enhance our experience, which in turn enhances our tonal, and allows us to move in higher frequencies. It's all self-relating.

The formula designed to do this, allows us to absorb or attract Prana into our being. It also allows us under this system to have clear thought and wax on, wax off training to discipline ourselves. It has a variety of ways to work with us.

What we're going to do is to first discuss chakras, which come from Hinduism and Vedic teachings. A chakra point is a focus point on the human body. We have a nervous system, which is like wires or routing that runs through our bodies. At some point these wires crisscross: a chakra point.

There are thousands of chakra points on the body. There are thousands of them—minor and greater ones.

As we selectively work our way to get to the primary chakra points, we encounter seven of them, which are like a straight line from the top of our head down. It's likened to a pole that goes through the top of our head down into the floor.

Our main chakra is our *crown chakra*, which is above our head, although some people say it's on our head. The next chakra point is what is called the *mind chakra*, or some people in other cultures refer to it as the third eye. It basically rests in-between our eyebrows, about a half an inch higher.

The third chakra is our *throat chakra*. Again, there are different opinions as to where specifically it rests; if we feel where our Adam's apple is, go down about three inches and this is our throat chakra. The next chakra will be our *heart chakra*, which is in the center of our chest about three inches above our solar plexus.

A lot of people believe the solar plexus, where the bridges of our breast plates meet, is a chakra point. It could be, but it's not necessarily a true chakra point. It has its uses, but we're not going to go there in this particular class. It doesn't serve our purpose.

The next chakra is about two inches below the belly button—the *chi chakra*. Chi is discussed in many forms of martial arts, or Ki energy in some pronunciations. This is where martial artists draw a lot of their energy up through their body in order to focus to perform certain physical feats.

Next, the *groin chakra* is in the actual groin area. Again, it's our lower chakra drawing energy up through the body. It is also the point where we probably have the most attention given because it's a sexual organ, so we have a lot of awareness that goes there.

Last, but not least, is one of the more powerful chakras called our *root chakra*. It is also called the Kundalini chakra, located at the very base of our tail-bone. Some people believe it's the tail-bone tip itself. It's not.

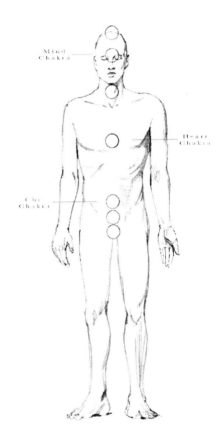

The seven primary chakras.

The Kundalini chakra is likened to a snake; they see the snake working its way up the spine.

In this particular case, we're not perceiving it as an actual snake; it symbolizes when energy moves; it slowly works its way up our spines and we can feel its heat. This is where the energy sits and rises up through the rest of the body. When it rises, of course it activates all the other chakras because it's passing through their vicinities.

Again, a chakra point is where all these nerves, or railroad tracks, begin to crisscross. The larger ones are where a lot of these lines crisscross; the main hub.

Imagine two railroad tracks where they crisscross, a minor intersection. When four or five tracks crisscross, this is considered a medium intersection. However, there is a hub where all tracks converge and are turned slowly so the lines depart in another direction; this is a master point. The railroad tracks represent what these chakra points are in our bodies. These are the ones we want to work with.

***

The groin chakra is a very powerful chakra point because its the acceptor and giver of life for male and female. Therefore, a lot of energy radiates there. Desirable energy radiates in this area and a lot of flow can move in and out. It's the only one that the non-practitioner, in the beginning, has ever focused their mind on. It has a lot of natural energy, more so than the others because of the amount of thought most people already give to that area.

However, the groin chakra is not going to serve us to get us to where we need to be. Its energy is very rooted in this dimension. We're trying to move beyond this dimension. Our focus should be on higher energies.

For Multi-Dimensional Meditation, the starting point is our Chi chakra, the one just below our belly buttons. When we meditate on it, it draws energy from the groin and root chakra, upward. We don't have to start with our lower points and focus on them. We can start from the one just below our belly button and it triggers the others to work and bring their energy up.

It's like a foundation energy; therefore, we always start from our foundation. We'll see this repeated in most things taught. We need something to put our feet on, so we can lift something over our heads.

We can't be on water; it's not a very good foundation if we're going to lift something over our heads. When we're going to support this energy field, we want a lower energy supporting all of our higher energies moving through us, so we always concentrate on that particular point first.

Moving on from there, we're going to move up to our heart chakra. That is the next step in the meditation. Don't worry about trying to meditate now; I will give a better step-by-step process later. Right now, let us discuss the overall method. The heart chakra really represents a lot of positive energy, happiness. This is where the concept of *have some heart* comes from. It is the part of us that heals the psyche, emotional wounds, and it releases the emotional pain in our life. It brings in what I call the *flower of blossoming*. It keeps repeating this expression of love and happiness.

So, when we think about this chakra point, we should always support it with a simple thought of happiness, and pleasurable positive thoughts. In doing so, it magnifies that vibration through our energy fields. We're basically feeding it good vibrations and in return it expands these vibrations like a flower, giving us a thousand happy vibrations all over.

Whenever we focus on this chakra point, we smile and when we're meditating we have a smile on our faces because it invokes gladness. Try it right now. Think about how you feel, then take a deep breath in and smile really big. Show some teeth! Put a big smile on your face. How does it make you feel? Smiling tells the sensory of our bodies to send a warm tingle through, releasing endorphins into our brains; that's what we want. We want to send messengers to our brain to yell out, "Hey, it's time to feel great! Let's have a party!"

We want to encourage this because it's an endorphin that's balancing all of our emotions. It removes the aura of depression, teaching the brain to clean its act up and throw the bad emotions out the door. Then we fill this space up with something worthwhile; we choose what we want to fill it with.

What we're going to fill it with is joyous energy, blissfulness. When we meditate, the happier we can be, the more it's going to amplify. It's like coding it into our system. Once we're done with our meditation, we go through life, and everybody wonders: *why is that person so happy?* We just feel good.

People who have a lot of heart energy, are people we can't dislike. Did you ever meet a person who was so nice and had something special about them? It is nothing they do or say; you just like them.

It's a vibration about them; they naturally have this heart energy, this favorable place where they emanate from. They are used to feeding and encouraging their good nature, trying to stimulate this good vibration even if they do it artificially by wearing a fake smile. Eventually, it becomes a real smile. That's the key. It becomes a real feeling.

We have to choose to invoke it to exercise it like a muscle to become strong. That's what we're going to do when we meditate on the heart chakra.

Working up, we're going to go to the throat chakra, which represents health and well-being. A lot of our glands are in our neck. These glands are chemical factories with a huge effect on the biochemistry of our brains and bodies; how we feel, and what makes us happy; and what makes us sad, what makes us feel tense and frustrated.

A lot of it has to do with these glands in our throat area. The signals in the vibration coming from there work for our health by telling everything else how it should get along: our organs, kidneys, livers, and bladders. When we focus on this chakra, we focus on a sense of well-being, a sense of health.

We are really telling these glands in our bodies to start doing their job correctly, to start refining this particular area of our bodies, and to do something that's balancing. Although, we don't have to say this to the body. It already knows what it needs to do, but sometimes it gets a little sluggish and when we focus on this chakra, we give it a bit of an electric jolt. It shocks it a little so it starts making everything run correctly.

Let's think about something. When we think about a spot, by having pure thoughts and giving it attention, it is like electricity traveling there suddenly. So, we can think about what it is to be in the spot. If we want to look at it in a physiological way, we're giving it electricity solely by thinking about this spot. The longer we think about it, the more we're stimulating electricity in that region.

The same goes for any other chakra. There's a method to the madness.

For the next and final chakra in the meditation, we turn our attention to our mind chakra. The mind chakra is very mental; it is the reasoning of our mind. The particular area we have to remember is the front of our skull area. Behind this is our frontal lobe, and that's what separates us from animals. It's what advanced the human race significantly beyond other animals.

The *pineal gland* is behind this area. In this region is the core, some people believe it's the seat of the soul. Similar to the seat of a car versus the rest of the car—the passenger seating, all the machinery, everything—whoever sits in the driver's seat is the driver of the vessel.

Who we are as energy beings—our Middle Pillar, which we really are—resides among all the chaos in our minds, and is believed to sit and operate in that particular region of the mind, or that region of the brain.

When we meditate, we give energy to this spot. We give electricity to this spot. Again, it's like taking an old dusty blanket or carpet on the floor, pulling it up, and shaking it out. All the dust made it look grey and the patterns of this beautiful carpet were barely seen. However, when we shake it out, all of a sudden we see the beautiful oranges, greens, violets, and blues; it looks like peacock feathers.

This is what's happening inside of this part of the mind. We never think to stimulate it with some thought, electricity, or energy. By thinking, it shakes it up a bit, like waking it up. This is why we focus on this particular spot.

It is going to, in some ways, help us improve our reading ability, mathematical ability, scholarly mental processing, and memory. Somehow, it's connected to all these areas and as we begin stimulation, it works its way to other regions of the brain, enhancing them.

By thinking about it, new neurons are built, like new fibers. Cells begin to grow, giving us more electrical discharges in our brain so we can calculate faster or think clearer. When focusing on this area, we're literally enhancing the biological part of our bodies as much as the energy field of our bodies.

It's always working on many different levels. Also, we can say psychic abilities, telepathy, sensory, and out-of-body experiences, are all empowered through the invocation or the ability to fire up the recesses of our minds.

At some point, we'll go into a class about all this, which explains how to develop all these abilities, what to do, and little techniques. It's all really very amazing.

Those are the three chakras we will use in Multi-Dimensional Meditation. The chi, heart and mind chakra.

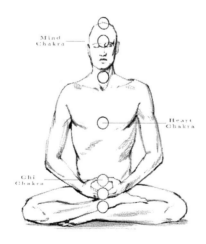

The three chakras used for Multi-Dimensional Meditation.
The Chi, the Heart and the Mind.

Focusing on the mind chakra continues to pull energy up from the heart chakra through the throat chakra but it doesn't stop there. It flows up to the crown chakra, which is very important because in some Hindu texts they always show this big purple or pink lotus flower over the head in their paintings, causing one to wonder: *Why is this flower over their head? Why is the stem of this flower going into their head?*

To explain it in modern language, so it makes sense, is to simply switch it. Instead of a lotus flower over our heads, imagine a big satellite dish towards the universe, the sky. Instead of a root sticking into our heads from the stem, we'll fix it with a coaxial cable that's plugged into our brain and into the satellite dish.

What does this tell us immediately? There's something coming from the heavens, sky, and universe; some kind of hidden information beyond our normal sense of hearing, sight, smell, and taste—something we're trying to bring in. What they were saying in the Hindu culture was it represented the sunlight and universal knowledge. The lotus flower brings in the sunlight, it absorbs it, and pulls universal knowledge into the person. This is what they are trying to say. It's the same thing; it's from a different perspective.

When we meditate solely on our crown chakra and we're only thinking about that, it's stimulating something in some other region of our brains that goes down to the pineal gland area, but different regions. It gives us some knowledge of who or what we need to know.

A person may say, "I need to be enriched with some kind of deeper understanding."

When a person opens up in this way, they are opening up to allow this to happen for it to come in. It means opening this channel to receive from God, or the universal consciousness.

Then the person is ready to say, "I'm willing to listen and experience whatever information you're trying to send me."

Now that we have an understanding of these seven chakras in a very healthy basic structure, we have to ask ourselves several questions. When we think of Prana and we think of chakra points, there is a connection there. There is a system that unites the Prana, the blue energy, and chakra points, which gets into the secret to this meditation.

Most schools of meditation simply instruct students to think of a color on their chakra point, or think of it as a sound. Sometimes in the United States, we have a tendency to create a candied effect; we twist information to create our own pretty little concept of it.

The real texture of what it was supposed to mean is lost, the real meaning behind it. At that time, meditation was presented so students would have the best results. So, why would they throw in all this other stuff, such as crystals?

When we meditate on a chakra, the secret is to take the middle and index fingers of whichever hand we want to use and simply place it on our chakra. While we have it now on our chakra, there's only one thing we need to do, and that is to pay attention to our fingers touching that spot.

It may sound like a simple thing to do, but after we do it for a few minutes, our minds tend to wander. The point is: the longer we can pay attention to our fingers touching that spot, what's happening is we're arcing this energy. Meaning, the blue and red energy is everywhere. In order to get the blue energy, we almost have to change our electrical current in our bodies to attract it.

We change our frequency a bit because we're so out of tune. We're so far from being in tune spiritually, we have to work with our bodies to receive what we need.

Remember the old televisions that were black and white? They had rabbit ears long before cable television. We'd get one, two, or three stations that overlaid each other—somebody would be walking in the background then we'd see something else in another screen.

Then as we approached the television to move the rabbit ears, what would happen? The television would become clear, then once we'd step back, the image would go really bad again. So, we'd have to find ways to get it exactly the way we wanted it.

As we touch our chakra and think about what it feels like, electricity is giving us data. The data sends bits of light back and forth through our nervous systems so quickly with the speed of light, that if we could see it, it would look like a golden thread of electricity wavering there.

When this happens, we change our electrical field and begin to blend frequencies that are mismatched like all those channels. We get a solid channel, one specific channel, and the blue light of this energy—Prana, all of a sudden starts to move towards you.

Little bits of blue, gentle light from around the room begins to absorb into us. It falls, like rain, into our bodies, or moves like meteorites toward us. Tiny specks of blue are what's cascading down. This is how we absorb the fuel needed to do things later; we need to absorb Prana into our bodies.

It's so fine we can't really see it. We have to think of the principles at first before we can really experience the true magnitude of what we are becoming.

The trick is to touch that particular chakra because when we touch, electrons are stimulated. Electrons are energy moving to our brains, telling us what we are feeling. Paying attention to it creates an electrical vortex; however, when we remove our hands from it, the vortex collapses, the channels become fuzzy again.

Do we lose what we collected? No. We keep what we collect. It's like a reservoir.

As we meditate, we're building stock or nourishment in our bodies, which we will later dispense for what we want it to do. If our minds wander away from touching the heart chakra, we begin to experience the Babbler, which in itself stops the threading.

At this point, the frequency is lost. It parallels letting go of the rabbit ears when we start thinking: *I have to do laundry.* Then we must refocus. As we refocus, we become aware of this spot again, so the threading resumes. This electrical light is part of our consciousness paying attention to this one spot, and, again, the blue light begins to move toward us.

When we do this on each chakra, we absorb Prana, but there's another little trick to this. We'll call this Exhibit A. Imagine a little circle on a piece of paper. In the center of the paper, we're going to make a half dollar size circle. Now, on the outside of this circle we're going to make a giant circle that goes around it. This represents our chakra point.

Below this chakra point, we're going to make another circle, so we're going to have three circles. As I mentioned earlier, we do not meditate on all seven chakra points. We meditate *strictly* on three. I say strictly because I have learned over the years students will be tempted to dabble with some other chakra to see what will happen. They will assume that after twenty plus years of teaching, I may have missed something, or there is a way to improve it. Go ahead and dabble. Burn your time and energy to your hearts content. When you realize how right I am, and that I gave you the best way to begin with, come back to get some real work done. If I thought there was any better way, I would be showing it to you. This is truly the best course of action.

Therefore, meditate strictly on the Chi chakra (just below our belly buttons), heart chakra, and mind chakra between our eyes (the third eye chakra). These are the only three on which we meditate.

The one we meditate on first is always the lower chakra, where the Chi resides. We want to pull the lower energy in this powerful chakra point up to enhance the other two chakra points. When we're finished with this area, it doesn't matter whether we go to the heart or mind chakra.

What we will find is, with all the other chakra points below, above, or in-between, different chakra points will bleed their energy into the other two. We're still getting the benefits of the other two without having to spend a lot of time focusing on that chakra.

Remember, this system has many systems designed within. We only have so much time in the day. Why practice multiple kinds of meditation, for hours each day (as many people do), when we could shorten our time and walk away with the equivalent of five hours worth of meditation work in one thirty-minute meditation using this method.

The energy of these chakra points will work into the other chakra points. Don't worry about getting or not getting them. More specifically, don't worry about the sexual chakra point; it's already so powerful, we don't even need to. Trust me, okay?

All of these things have been considered already. Simply listen to what I am saying, apply the method for as long as you want, and reap the rewards.

When we meditate, we attract Prana from the outside. When it touches our body's field of energy, the blue light starts to penetrate us; it gets a program. The best way to describe this is to think of fossil fuel. What is fossil fuel? It's gasoline, petroleum, diesel fuel . . . it goes on.

This fuel comes from one source, which is manufactured or created to become something very specific. It can only be used in certain machinery, in certain ways. Other machinery can't use it.

When we meditate on our heart chakra, the Prana that enters us receives the frequency we've created. Remember, we need to be happy and smile because it's going to enhance this chakra.

In essence, the energy asks, "What is it that I need to become? What is it that I need to be in you?"

So, we give it a program and it fills us with this positive, high, beautiful energy. It radiates in us. If we meditate on our lower chakra, we bring in the Prana. That lower chakra is going to give us more of a solid energy and ensure our energy fields stay nice and tight, and doesn't flutter around.

By meditating on our lower chakra, we're teaching our energy to stay in. We're empowering our foundation; it's more of a physical energy. This is why martial artists use it because it's the energy used for physical strength, endurance, or athleticism. It's something we all need to feel psychologically good to get through the day.

We're getting physically tired and sleepy too easily, or we're not feeling we have enough get up and go. We lack the encouragement to get up in the morning to meditate, or meditate later on in the day. If we meditate on this, we give our bodies energy, helping to encourage our minds to do the other meditations. This is why the lower chakra is an important spot.

The mind chakra, of course, is going to convert it into a psychic energy. In either case, it's going to enhance all our abilities so we can read better or faster. Not only are we stimulating this part of the brain, but we're giving ourselves fuel to do the things that go beyond simple mental things, such as reading and writing.

What meditation on this chakra will also do is to enhance our ability to feel what other people feel; psychically know something before it happens; or experience deja vu, knowing something has happened to a loved one. It's this part of the brain that's been stimulated; it's like a twitching muscle, a freak event for a split second. What we're doing is stimulating this area and giving it much fuel. Immediately, we'll begin to feel all these paranormal abilities we weren't aware of before. Our sensory increases. Therefore, when we meditate on the mind chakra, we better be prepared because this is something that may result from it.

This is, in part, how the sixth sense is developed. By clearing the mind, one learns to focus. The sixth sense is a natural sense above the normal five. Therefore, we're giving it attention, more or less. If we were to concentrate purely on touching, we would be able to have a greater level of sensation or feeling. By focusing in on a sense, or giving it full attention, it will amplify.

If we were to hone in or train a lot on sight, as a master artist, we would see different hues of color, and visual textures better than if we were merely glancing over things, or not giving it extensive attention.

What will happen is, if it's not used for paranormal abilities, it will simply enhance our minds. All the electrons in our brains will be enhanced to create better performing minds, better performing brains.

If our goal is not to develop spiritually or psychically, that's not going to be forced on us. By the same token, if this development is something we want, we can propel it into this direction greatly. If we choose to go there we can, using the proper knowledge sources to learn how to do so.

When meditating, I feel Prana more in my mind chakra than the other two chakras. Why is this?

We will gravitate to what's our natural chakra. For many people, it is the mind chakra. If we bowl, the bowling ball will naturally either hit to the left or right because of our natural body position.

Do you consider yourself to be more cerebral, or tend to contemplate a lot about things mind-related? If you tend to spend a lot of time cerebrally, with greater mental focus, you're gravitating to this area as your natural focus.

Most people, when they find they get a lot more Prana in certain chakra points than in others, tend to want to spend more time there, which makes it more dominant. Therefore, it becomes a self-feeding cycle. It isn't something we can automatically change. It's very natural for our inner-mind, inner-navigator to be drawn there. It's the center of our main strength.

Consider this: why do people use their left arm versus their right arm, or vice versa? If they are right-handed, they naturally use their right hand more often than the left; although each arm works relatively the same. If people are left-handed, just the opposite applies. In this case, they will use different centers.

Particular chakra points are going to come more naturally without thinking about it. If we find, at some point, one chakra is stronger than others, consider ceasing meditation on the stronger chakra for the next two to four weeks to focus on the other two. In other words, let's exercise our left arms and place less emphasis on our right arm. The end result is a more balanced meditation. More than likely, we'll have our most powerful breakthroughs at that point.

We may, however, find ourselves resisting this balance. When we feel drawn to one chakra, it's going to feel really good to focus on it. We won't want to spend time on the others. At some point, we will question why we need to spend time on the others.

If a little time feels that good, more is better right? The answer is not completely clear cut. We could be listening to a piece of music, a symphony, and the one thing we focus on is a violin or trumpet. It's something we gravitate toward; we put our mental focus on that one instrument.

It's very important to acquire a taste outside of what is natural for us. Forcing ourselves to experience something, at first feels very unnatural; there's resistance. What will happen is we will acquire a taste for it. We adapt, we start to learn to appreciate it in greater ways.

Some people may have the same experience drinking wine. They may have not liked wine at all; however, they tasted different wines. Eventually they started to acquire a taste for it, then a wider range to continue to acquire a broader taste.

When we learn to bring in, or harmonize more instruments, although they are not ideal instruments we gravitate toward, in the end it's the entire symphony that's going to move us to a height no single instrument could have fully taken us on its own, at least in that way.

Naturally, I'm drawn to focusing on the mind chakra. However, my greatest breakthroughs aren't necessarily when I meditate with the mind chakra. These sudden advancements were while meditating with the heart chakra or my lower chakra. In nearly twenty years, my experiences with other very intellectual students have been very similar.

Another thing that may turn us away, at least from the lower chakra, is some people experience involuntary twitches on the lower chakra. We don't experience this sensation with the mind or heart chakra.

Most of the time we associate this with energy blocks. Also, our muscular system is going to react to electrical impulses naturally. What's happening is we're tapping into our Prana energy or shifting it around. We're awakening areas we normally wouldn't venture into; they are foreign to us. Therefore, some quirks will need to be worked out.

Lately, I've been doing sit-ups using a sit-up machine. It looks horrible, but I have to go through the pain for the gains. Early on, I experienced energy twitching. Usually, this involuntary jerking may be associated with Kundalini yoga or various kinds of energy working through the system.

Always remember we are not only mental and spiritual, but also physical: mind, body, spirit. There's a reason we were created this way. The best approach to ward off twitching is to do some stretches to prepare physically to better cope with and adjust to energy movements moving through our bodies.

The bottom line is energy is very real. It's coming from a different dimension and we're tuning ourselves into it. It's going to run on very similar nervous system lines as our nervous system relates to muscle expansion and retraction. It's going to react to the thinking it's the same signal, but it's not.

Until it learns through trial and error, we're going to have to unfortunately go through a few of these experiences, but they will pass. Most of it can be subsided with some basic stretches before actually engaging in meditation.

The point is, when Prana comes into us, it is converted into a specific energy according to which particular chakra point we're touching. It changes the frequency as it moves into us to have a specific goal, job, or orientation.

We've covered energy and these points. Now, we want to take a little step outside of our normal form of meditation and move into another concept.

There are different kinds of meditation in life. We can walk and go into a certain state of mind as we discussed before. We can sit at a beach and listen to the crashing of waves. It's meditation. We can sit in a park and find a certain centering. These are good forms of meditation.

What we have to pay attention to is certain things that make sense, but don't make sense at the same time. We'll find the worst enemy we have is the Babbler. When the Babbler starts thinking, we have to learn to quiet our minds and bodies. When we suddenly find ourselves talking again, we need to focus on harnessing this energy, be quiet, relax, and be still.

We don't want to feed the Babbler because it's empowering the Babbler. We're training ourselves to react a certain way. We do not want to be upset with ourselves because we're babbling and talking. Why feed the frustration?

What we'd rather do is simply focus on being silent. In some way, this is a good thing that's happening because something inside of us recognizes we're trying to achieve something wondrous. This is how we have to look at it and treat ourselves.

Eventually, we're going to find the Babbler over time gets quieter and stops. It will take less time away from what we're trying to achieve or where our minds need to be.

Sometimes, I'm unaware how long I've drifted until at some point I realize it got me, again!

We have to realize the Babbler for what it is. If we truly boil it down and accept it for what it is, the Babbler is a necessity. It's a necessary thing! Most people aren't white cells, the vast majority are red cells. This is an integrated natural, organic consciousness designed to ensure the organism functions on the planet, does what it's supposed to do—procreates, functions, experiences, and survives.

It's there as a necessity. It's strongly hot-wired into all of our biological consciousnesses. It's embedded into our organic cells.

When we get frustrated or start thinking about shutting down the Babbler, consider: *is there some simple way to do it?* This has been a battle for thousands of years. Since man began to contemplate self, there has been contention with the Babbler.

If we incorporate going for a walk, preferably outdoors under healthy conditions, or even on a treadmill, the brain has a tendency to work out all its issues, thoughts, contemplations, and pressures. All of the things demanded of us in a modern society, we didn't have to deal with thousands of years ago. At least, they weren't as demanding as they are today.

A walk has its own way of releasing stress. After that walk, come home, sit down, and prepare to go into meditation, particularly for people who have the hardest time with the Babbler. It may not be ideal for everybody, considering their health or physical capabilities, but for those who can go for a simple walk, the results will be surprising.

It's not something we have to always incorporate before meditation. We may need to do it for a while until we can simply sit down and get to where we need to be.

Once we've trained the brain to unwind, we're able to go to that place more often without as much interference. Another angle we may find a bit quirky is to sit down and have a conversation with the Babbler. Yes, sit down and hear the Babbler out. The end result is we will begin to tire of the Babbler.

Something happens psychologically that serves as an affirmation or confirmation, mentally. It tends to reduce the effects of the Babbler.

Diet is also a big one. If we're going to drink coffee, tea, or any kind of stimulants, or eat anything with a lot of sugar, it's going to stimulate the body. The Babbler is different states of consciousness in our bodies.

We've got several of them straddling for position:

There's one who says, "I'm hungry."

Another one says, "I want to rest and lay down."

Another consciousness comes forward to say, "You know, I don't like the buzzing and the sounds and they're annoying me from outside."

They're all present as survival mechanisms dating back to evolutionary consciousness. What we want to do is simply sit down and acknowledge all of them.

We must acknowledge, "I know we have to deal with this. I know this has been an issue."

We can start acknowledging through the lists of things in our minds by writing them down on paper. It may add an extra five or ten minutes before we meditate, but we'll be surprised at how we are self-trained to mentally respond to these exercises.

Another thing is we may want to think of a mirror to see an image of ourselves. We can focus on our image and tell ourselves the Babbler looks like us, but it's who has been talking and we accept it's not us. In our minds, we recognize this image represents the Babbler and we shatter it.

What we're trying to do is bring forward our true self. By doing so, we're giving ourselves the advantage of saying we want some quiet time. "This is a necessary thing and I demand to have it."

These are just a few countermeasures to tackle constant thinking, which hinders successful meditation. However, the biggest challenge to meditation is diet.

We need to watch what we're eating and drinking. We, particularly, need to avoid introducing too many stimulants to our bodies because they facilitate different Babblers to become empowered. We want to ensure we are not empowering them too much.

Sometimes people say they're sore, or they experience muscle aches trying to achieve a *proper* meditation. If we are struggling and sore, we aren't meditating.

We need to focus on meditation first, everything else second. Meaning, sit in a chair, try to keep our back straight, yet be comfortable.

Keep in mind: we will always have the Babbler. People who meditate and have meditated for years still encounter challenges with the Babbler. Remember one thing: we're always gaining ground, gaining Prana. There's no such thing as a bad meditation. If for only one second we are able to clear our minds to think about this spot, we have probably gained more energy than most people, who don't understand these principles, will ever get.

Now, taking everything into consideration, as we meditate under this system and build energy, the first thing we're learning is to control and relax ourselves. There are a series of steps we want to take when we meditate.

The first thing is to choose whether we're going to sit on the floor in a half lotus or if we're going to sit in a chair of some type. A half lotus is _not_ a full lotus where both heels of our feet are brought up on top of our thighs. In a half lotus, one leg is pulled underneath, Indian-style while the other is lifted on top of it into a position that feels comfortable.

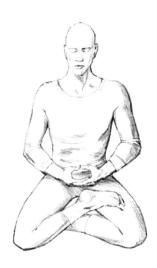

Half-lotus is the best meditation position. One foot resting on a leg with a straight posture.

We want to try to sit with a straight posture. When we slouch, energy isn't moving up and down our spine because this is where the energy moves in our bodies.

Go ahead and sit now as if you were about to meditate. Choose either the relaxed Indian-style, with both ankles touching the floor, a half lotus where one ankle is resting against the opposite thigh, or find a chair to sit in with a straight back. When sitting in a chair, it is important to not cross the legs; rather keep them straight and parallel.

For those of us who have terrible posture, we can relax our shoulders. There's no need to keep them so upright. We need to relax them and our chests. No one said when we have a straight back, we have to keep everything so firm and tight. No one's saying our backs have to be perfectly straight. It's okay for our posture to be a bit relaxed. As we meditate, it's probably not going to be so perfect. Don't worry about it.

The number one thing we have to be largely concerned about is paying attention to touching our chakra point. Are we still aware of the touch or have we become too involved in how our bodies are sitting? Are we so focused on whether or not we're bending, leaning, or tilting that we have lost our sense of where the sensory of our chakra point is? Our main mission? Whatever the case, it's something we want to keep in mind.

Next, lets examine our hands. We want to have one hand down, resting on our feet below our belly area. If sitting in a chair, it should be resting in our lap. We want the other hand to lay on top of the first hand. Then we're going to touch our two thumbs at the tips. This is a proper way to rest our hands for our energy.

The proper way to rest hands during meditation.

Naturally, this may sound like a contradiction because we're considering how we are going to touch our chakra point if our hands are sitting down in this position. Eventually, we're going to grow out of having to touch our chakra points. We're going to have to think about it and visualize a seed exists there; there's a pressure.

We'll be able to concentrate our minds well enough that we will no longer need to touch it. How long will this take? That can take anywhere from three to six months, or even a year. It's different for each person; some chakra points may be easier for us to focus on than others. No one is saying we can't reach out and touch it while we're focusing with our eyes closed then put our hands back down.

We need to keep our minds on the spot. It doesn't matter what our bodies are doing. These are simply enhancements, but it doesn't mean it's going to prevent us from achieving a good meditation by moving our bodies around a bit.

One of the things we want to note is the position our hands and feet are in. Our energy is cycling around our stomach and chest areas, down to the palms of our hands and back up to our heart chakra region and down again. There's a certain kind of warmth in this region.

This is energy that's being told to remain there, by our hands in this position. As we're meditating, we're gathering energy and it's pooling it into our bodies.

What we get into is subtle energy. For example, it's where we feel something but we're not exactly sure. It takes some mental effort to become aware of it, so it takes practice. It doesn't mean we're going to feel this way right away, so don't be upset if it isn't felt immediately.

However, if we take our hands and sit with our hands in the proper position, resting on top of each other in our laps, we may be able to feel a subtle heat if we can be aware of it. Then take our hands and move them away from our bodies, resting them onto our knee caps. This is the position many people think of when they imagine meditation. If we pay attention to this same area, we'll feel a coolness move in there as if the energy has just moved into a different position. It's no longer swelling in that area or gathering.

If we put our hands back into the position, palm into hand, we'll notice warmth begins to build up in this region very gently in a few seconds. Women tend to feel it a bit faster than men in some cases because women are more sensitive in this way than men.

Open our hands again by placing them on the knees; then pay attention to how they feel. Also, take a breath and we should feel this shift because breathing is very connected to energy, as we'll discover momentarily.

As we bring our hands back together in our laps, we'll, again, feel the swelling. Can you feel the difference? If not try it again after practicing the meditation for several weeks. The more aware you are of your energy the more obvious it is. Being aware of these subtle things will help us in the end. It's what gathers our mental strength to move our minds into higher regions.

Meditating with hands in this position allows energy to gather at a faster rate.
It cycles and flows in a tighter circuit through the chakras.

Meditating with hands in this position breaks the energy circuit. Like a door left open, energy does not cycle and flows away from the body.

If it makes sense to us, we can feel something, or if it's something we can reciprocate, we realize we can work with this because it's something we can understand in a physical way. If we have this awareness as we're doing something spiritual at the same time, it's more encouraging.

At this point, we can rest our hands and arms. In fact, why don't we take our feet out of this position and put one sticking out. Suppose we were meditating and needed to stretch our legs out. What is the most important thing? The touch, staying focused on our chakra point.

Feel the chakra point. We don't ever want to get our minds off of it. If a dragon were in the neighborhood and we were trying to wrestle it down, we would want to hang on to it! We don't want to let go because if it's flying through the air, we don't want to fall off. You have to hang on to that sucker! We don't want to let go of our chakra point and where our minds are.

We automate the body with our eyes shut, hands in position very easily. We take the leg we need to stretch out and put it out. Staying focused, then we take the other leg, if it needs stretching, and put it out. We can do this while we are meditating, to alleviate any distraction coming from our legs if they fall asleep. Stretch them out; keep meditating.

The hands usually aren't too demanding because we work with them all the time. We don't need to think about what we're doing. This gets back into the first class about keeping non-thought. Do we need to think about everything we do, or can we think without thought?

If our legs are bothering us, we don't need to think of them bothering us, about what we're going to do with them, or what other people are going to think. This is not going to help us with our energy.

All that matters is to throw them out. Get into a position that feels comfortable, but stay on top of focusing on the spot; try to maintain non-thought.

Then, once our legs have stretched out and they feel good enough, we don't want to remain in the position. We want to bring them back into position and continue our meditation. If we have to do this ten times during our meditation then so be it. It will get easier in time.

The bottom line is this. The reason why we're in the half lotus position is because it's a very good way to maintain our energy fields. It's a good way to pool the energy we are talking about. It's a greater rather than a lesser advantage.

When we meditate, we harness more energy faster in this position than if we stretch out our legs. Then we'll lose 25–50 percent of the Prana we're harnessing. So, we want to stay in this position.

If we take our legs from the half lotus and simply move them to sit Indian-style, we'll find the support of our bodies feel very different. It's seemingly not as supportive. Remember we're always talking about the spine and energy moving up and down it. Those of us who have bad posture don't even want to try to sit Indian-style because it's not helping us.

If we go back into lifting our foot into a half lotus, we will find that we suddenly have this extra support. The only problem with it is because it's unnatural for us; we're not used to it. The muscles are going to get a bit sore and become somewhat achy. The more we do something, our bodies accept it.

There have been cases when people have taken two years to get used to it; however, some people adapt in two hours. Everybody is different. One of the things we can do is to take our two feet out and bring the heels together, so they're about a foot away from our bodies. We can choose the length, whatever feels comfortable. Never do something that hurts; move into a position that feels comfortable.

What we're going to do is take our hands, put them on our knee caps, and lift them up and down like bird wings. Most people will feel a certain pressure, more or less, in their inner thighs, which is actually a tendon. It's similar to a very tight elastic band.

As we begin to stretch it, it actually becomes flexible and healthier than if it's tight. What will happen is, if we do this often, while we're sitting, or even while we're meditating, we may want to let our legs lie in this position.

Sometimes even resting our hands can feel pretty tight there. If we want to tighten them up even more, we can pull the inner legs and our feet in toward our groin to a certain point. Again, we don't want to hurt ourselves. We just want to bring it to a certain point where we can barely tolerate it. Then, once more, put our hands in the same position and keep working it.

Eventually, we're going to loosen those areas up; so when we go to sit in a half lotus, we'll find it's almost more relaxing immediately. It feels more comfortable because we're stretching it. Before we start our meditation this may be something we want to do. We're going to also cover meditating in a chair compared to sitting on a floor because meditating in a half lotus is not ideal for everybody. We have to have options and certainly want to put them out there. The full lotus can be very good for some people and I'm not saying don't use it. Find a practical method that's not excessive.

We're using a system that uses the best universal system to gain the most advantage in meditation. If people are struggling now to do a full lotus, it becomes such a distraction mentally for some people, they simply abandon their meditation.

There is no definitive advantage to do a full lotus that a person cannot get from a half lotus, which is easier to do. Likewise, there's is no definitive percentage of more Prana being gained because there's better support for the back in a full lotus than a half lotus.

So, we're going to do a half lotus because most people have trouble with the full lotus; it's difficult enough to do a half lotus. It's not so much it harnesses the energy, but it helps us support the back and spine areas. It keeps it a bit straighter, a bit firmer.

If we switch our legs into an Indian-style position, we'll feel we don't quite have as much back support. If we switch into a half lotus, it seemingly firms it up a bit, and sitting in a chair isn't really different either. It's a matter of preference.

My meditations are just so out there now that it's sometimes hard for me to relate to where other people are. Sometimes I'll sit in a half lotus two hours talking to people and notice their facial expressions as they try to sit in this half lotus to keep up with me. I've forgotten how uncomfortable it can be.

I'm trying to tell people I understand. Don't feel you have to sit in this position. It takes practice. You do a little each day and you'll be able to do it longer until eventually, like me, you won't think about it.

I was a wreck when I first started. I mean I had one leg that I couldn't get to go down—it was like a foot off the air. I thought: *my God, I look like a fool, I can't do this.*

I learned the stretch from a friend and in a matter of days, I realized a great difference! So any obstacle you have, can be overcome. Don't rush yourself, don't hurt yourself. That's the bottom line.

If we hurt ourselves then the pain is going to distract us from achieving our best meditations. It defeats the goal. We're not winning; we're now losing.

We can switch. If we can get used to sitting in a half lotus for some reason, it's a bit more preferential. However, what is the most important thing? The touch. Stay focused on the touch, so it doesn't matter about anything else.

Other people believe we should sit on the floor without anything supporting our backs. This is not advisable because the beginner's back is not used to supporting its weight, so it becomes very tired. Besides, a very strong, complaining Babbler, rather than a passive Babbler is a big enough problem.

What is the answer? Common sense dictates we lean up against a wall, or couch when seated on the floor. We need to find something to support our backs.

Eventually we're going to build these muscles whether we're using something or not. In some schools of thought, we will see even the best meditators with sheets tied up. We'd be surprised how much this actually supports their backs.

We're not less respectable as meditators by doing this. We're actually, in a sense, more respected because we're after the achievement, not how much we can discipline ourselves.

Now, of course, we may want to get to the point where we can sit on the floor and not have anything to lean up against. The reality is, it doesn't matter that we can't lean up against something. We can lean against something or we can sit in a chair.

The heart of what we're after is absorbing Prana. If we absorb enough Prana it's going to change and uplift our lives. It's going to be profound.

How fast does it take to get there? If one person is driving sixty miles per hour and another person is doing eighty miles per hour, and we have an eighty mile distance to travel, how much longer is it going to take the person doing sixty miles per hour versus the one doing eighty miles per hour to get there? Twenty minutes?

That's not significant enough to cause extreme discomfort or pain to our bodies. The point is if we practice a method each and every day, eventually we're going to get there. We may as well be doing light speed if the other person is not doing anything at all. What difference does it make? It's really about how much we want to attempt to achieve our goal.

We want to have a chair where our backs are supported, not a reclining chair. We don't want to be in a recliner, it isn't going to help you.

We want something that makes our back straight as we sit. We want to have our feet flat on the floor with our heels touching the floor. We do not ever want to

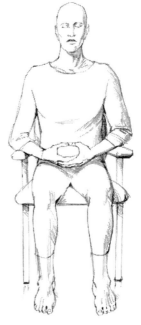

In a chair, sit with a straight back. Hands or legs should never cross.

cross our feet. In fact, we don't even want them to touch. They could be an inch or five inches apart, but we don't want them terribly far apart. Our hands can rest in the same position on our laps; that's perfectly okay.

A lot of people see pictures of people with their hands on their kneecaps. Simply sitting in a chair is the same thing. Focus on the same things that we've learned. It's no different than sitting on the floor, but we'll probably have more success if we find physically sitting on the floor is too demanding.

In the long run, we may want to exercise a little in our lives, so eventually we can work to sit in a position on the floor a bit more often. It's probably more traditional and custom because of where meditation's origins were. This is why there's this sense of needing to sit on the floor. There isn't a major difference if we sit in the chair. What *is* important is we never lie down and meditate.

It's very simple; it's common sense. If we lie down and we're stretched out on the floor, what is it we're really telling ourselves? We're telling ourselves to go to sleep; it's in that mode and an indirect way of suggesting something.

So, here we are trying to relax and go into this deep state of mind to have non-thought, and we're lying on the floor. Our first instinct is going to start to fall asleep, roll over, and snuggle into our arm and we're out. We don't want to stand up necessarily and meditate because we're telling ourselves what? Be awake, alert, and conscious.

The idea is to be in a sitting position with our back semi-straight because it tells us to relax and go into the sleeping state of mind. However, it's forcing us, in a sense, to almost be standing, yet halfway in-between, telling us to be a little conscious and alert.

It's a different level of consciousness that takes place. We're meeting the third road. We're meeting the third point, which is the ideal place for us to experience what it is we need to experience.

Let's talk about the basics. Our field of energy, when our legs are brought into a half lotus, is within a centered area.

It's like it's brought close to our bodies. When we are sitting in a chair our legs are extended several feet from us. When we're crossing our legs, the energy is like taking two wires and twisting them.

We're making a larger area where our energy is going to start together. With our legs crossed, we hold our energy close to our bodies. While sitting in a chair our energy flows to our bodies lowest point, the floor, where our feet are resting. Therefore, it stretches instead of condensing it, however it still collects in the reservoir area where we want it—in the main part or area of our bodies.

It's now being thinned out and we're not feeling the impact as quickly because a bigger pot takes longer to fill with water than a smaller pot. In some ways, by holding this energy in, it's a faster way to get it to reach a pitch or tone we want. Remember, we're not thinking in terms of quantity necessarily; these are analogies to help understand something very complex.

The first thing we do is either sit in a chair or on the floor. We want to choose a place that's quiet, a place we don't frequent very often. When we meditate, we don't want to be in a place where we'll be disturbed, or a place where we do a lot of thinking and have activities. We want to pick an obscure spot in our environment because it doesn't hold certain recognition in our minds as much as other places.

Instead of meditating in our living room, which would be the first location we may think, we may want to meditate on the kitchen floor by the wall, or in a bedroom. We want to select different kinds of situations; the point is, we want to meditate often in the spot we choose.

Choosing a spot is important and it should be chosen by what *feels* comfortable. It's not that we select a spot because it's the best place to not be disturbed. We may *need* to sit in a particular spot.

Have you ever been home alone and all of a sudden get this really strange feeling to lay down somewhere on the floor or sit in a very obscure spot? Nobody talks about it, but we find ourselves in some weird scenarios. It's the sense we'll feel better if we sit in this spot or lay on the floor, rather than on the couch or chair.

It's the same premise when we choose our spot to meditate. It's the spot where the energy feels right. We are energy beings. There's energy everywhere.

In chapter one, we covered energy and how it can affect us in our everyday life. Every place has a certain kind of feel or energy. So we find our spot; we meditate in it, drawing in Prana. The result is our energy field grows.

What is happening with this energy? It's like the floor is a sponge absorbing the good frequency we're working on.

When we get up and leave the spot, it radiates the vibration we had there because it absorbs it like a sponge. It doesn't have a mind of its own; it's open to whatever happens to it.

When we frequent our spot, what's happening? We're strengthening the vibration there. What's even more interesting is when we sit in our spot, it slingshots us faster to that familiar place so we can continue working from there.

If we go to a spot that's not familiar, we'll probably do well because we're well-trained; our energy is working. The spot holding our energy has a sense of how far we've explored. This is our spot, our power place. This is where we're going to be most powerful when we need to gather our strength. Of course, we'll want to sit there.

This is not to say we can't meditate out in nature, under a tree, over at a friend's house, or in a cabin while we're on vacation. In these situations, we're going to look for what? For instance, if it's at a park, we're going to take a panoramic view to find the quietest place. Then we're going to zoom in on our spot. Different spots offer different things as we'll discover.

Sitting under an old tree is a profound experience when we clear our minds. There's a different language between us and the tree when we approach it without thinking like a human being, or with conditions of how we expect it to communicate.

There's a vibration from the tree that works with you. It gives you wisdom, its wisdom, and you receive it because you're not putting any conditions on it.

When most people pray to God, they talk *at* God. When we meditate, we're listening to God. When we meditate under an old tree, we're opening ourselves to receive something it has to say (if there is intelligence behind this tree). We're intentionally clearing our minds to feel what it needs us to feel, or know what it's explaining to us.

If we're very calm, peaceful, and receptive it's going to share something with us. Whether or not we see it being constructed in terms in our minds, or we simply know something has changed about us. This is what matters.

If we go to a beach house, we're going to find the best spot. Naturally, we don't want to go out to the beach in mid-day sun because we'll have the heat and sunlight to contend with. Choose wisely—not just what feels good, but also what's environmentally friendly.

We don't want to meditate near water, necessarily, because water attracts mosquitoes. What happens if we become so distant from our bodies that when we bring ourselves out of this stage, we have bites all over us? We want to be conscientious and find environmentally safe places.

Rest assured, we're not going to be so out of our conscious bodies that we'll not sense danger. Our Babblers will emerge. If an insect bites, we'll swat while meditating. We'll know to do it, or this is not currently a comfortable position.

Which brings up another point, there will be times when we're meditating, the Babbler may attempt to distract us. We may feel all sorts of itching sensations that make no sense. If we ignore them, they'll fade away. Conversely, if we react to them, it will worsen because it realizes this is a way to distract us. This is something to definitely keep in mind.

We find our spot; we sit in our spot; we work in our spot; and it's the place we do our work. It's our power place. It's our main spot at home. Then we may find a place in the forest. We may also find a place at other friends' houses.

What about meditating with other people?
Should I meditate with a group?

The best meditations are done alone. I prefer not to meditate with other people. This may sound horrible, but people are at varying octaves and their energy is evolving in different places. When we're meditating with someone else, there tends to be a linking effect. We may begin to feel the energy places of the other people. In some ways, they don't allow us to enter where we need to go.

My students often ride my coattails. I drag them along. Of course, they're very eager to hop on. I don't mind. Sometimes, I take everybody for a ride. I'm willing to bring people out there, in-between, or to higher states of consciousness from time to time.

The point is, we do our best work by ourselves. It's not to say we shouldn't ever meditate with other people. I'll explain.

When we meditate with other people much like meditating with the old tree from our previous example, what's going to happen? We're going to gain knowledge from them. It's like a ringing wine glass. We know when we've hit the right pitch as our finger circles the wine glass. It's the same thing.

When we meditate with groups of people, we want to ensure they are friends, people with whom we feel comfortable. We never want to meditate with someone if we don't feel comfortable with them. If somebody does not belong, they just don't belong. This is not to say we can't be supportive of other people, but we've got to trust our feelings.

When we find the right group of people to meditate with, and we have meditations with the right harmony, it eventually becomes like a wine glass ring. We're going to benefit each other. It's going to become, instead of individual meditations, one group meditation. Where this meditation goes can be profound. What it shows us can be quite intense.

Usually the best meditators in the group will end up leading the pack. When people are good at meditating, there's no coattail riding. Everybody is doing their own work, following this energy path. It can be a very amazing thing.

It's a matter of preference one may experience from time to time. The more we learn about meditating, however we acquire this knowledge, it's our duty to help other people somehow, someday, someway with this information.

We can't always say, "I don't want to meditate with anybody else because it's all about what I'm getting out of it."

At some point, we will have to allow somebody to ride on our coattails to show them the way. We must remember, what we take or get from the Universe, we need to give to others from ourselves. The Universe will refill us more abundantly. This has always been my experience.

Now, let's move on to practical technique. First we need to find our spot. Once we're in our spot, we're going to sit and become aware, thinking about our bodies.

We will think about how our feet feel pressing against the floor; how our butt area feels sitting in the chair or on the floor. We're going to become aware of how our shirt feels on our chest; how our hair feels lying on the sides of our heads; how our lips feel, their tension or dryness.

We want to make ourselves think about how our bodies feel; how our hands feel touching against themselves lying in our lap; how our back feels pressing against whatever it may be touching.

Take two to three minutes thinking about this. The more we think about how our bodies feel, the more we're going to realize it's not us.

The same way we can reach out and touch a table and say, "That's not part of me; I recognize that."

You can reach out and touch the carpet and say, "This is something outside of me."

Everybody assumes their body is them. When we start to think about our bodies, it's like touching all these things saying, "This is a muscle; this is an organ; this is tissue, and this is a shirt."

It's a way of separating our minds from where we are. It allows us to find our spirit center, our consciousness. As we think about our bodies, acknowledge how our ears feel; feel how our cheeks weigh on our faces. Go into that place for two or three minutes. It begins to relax us. We begin to go into a certain place.

After we've done this for two or three minutes—there's no specific amount of time—we'll know when it's time to move on. Now, let's focus on the tip of our noses. Then the region just below our noses, or nostril area, and feel the air moving in. Then let's breathe out of our noses. Some people prefer not to; there's no problem with breathing out of our noses. Again, feel the air moving in.

For now, don't follow the air going through our noses, down our throats, into our chest, and back out. Don't follow it. Just concentrate on the simple in and out pattern. The feeling of the air going in and out on the tip of the nose. Let's keep our minds in this vicinity; this is all that matters. We'll develop our knack for it after awhile.

We're going to do this for about another two minutes. Gently breathe in, breathe out. Nice and slow; not too fast, not too slow. After we've breathed in this pattern for a few minutes, we're going to visualize Prana as blue, white, or silver light; whatever we want. If we think of it as a positive energy, that's all it will be.

We're breathing Prana into us. We know it's filling us up; it's filling some other part of us with this white light, this energy. This energy is going to exude from our entire body like an illumination. Like a light bulb, all of a sudden every pore of our skin will radiate. This light will be coming out of us as if it's cleansing us.

At this point, we have to be willing to be calm and still, acknowledging our flesh is not who we are. We sense this flesh is not who we are; it's separate. We can now move into a relaxed state of mind, breathing in and out the Prana. We're going to continue to follow this pattern of breathing it in, then breathing it out.

After we've done this for two or three minutes, we will simply know to move on. Now we'll take one hand and move it to just below our belly button; touching the Chi chakra. We're going to our lower chakra point and hold it there.

We're going to keep our eyes shut the entire time. Some people teach students to keep their eyes open to look at something. When people see things during meditation, they may become distracted, giving the Babbler more to work with.

Suddenly, we see the book in the corner we've been looking for nearly three months to find, or the watch, which has been missing for the past year under the television. Bottom line, we want to avoid excuses for the Babbler, so let's close our eyes.

Close our eyes, relax, feel our bodies, then breathe using our breathing system. We don't have to give it any more attention. Let's move our consciousness, or attention, to the lower chakra and feel it. Simply feel it; just be. No thought, just calm, relaxed, and at one with ourselves. We're going to experience what it is to feel this.

Don't worry about getting bored. It's amazing because we're collecting Prana; it's coming into our bodies. We may allow a visualization, knowing, or awareness of this energy moving inside of us. When we're relaxed enough, we release ourselves from this physical vibration.

Once we've learned to let our minds become clear enough to the point where we're so bored we've forgotten what it is to be bored—not thinking anything—our energy is going to shift and we're going to find we're not in the place we were before.

After we've meditated for about ten minutes per chakra point, it comes out to a thirty-minute meditation. We may prefer to start with three or five minutes, whatever we feel ready to do. The longer the meditation, the more Prana we will collect.

A good, healthy meditation takes about thirty minutes. After we meditate ten minutes on our lower chakra, we need to then choose to either move into our heart or mind chakra.

Move to that chakra and focus for another ten minutes. Again, relax, stay focused on the point, and feel the sensation.

We want to stay aware of that particular spot in our minds. Focusing on that specific chakra changes the frequency of the Prana coming into us. It's filling us and working in us. Now, let's switch to either our heart or mind chakra, whichever hasn't been worked with yet.

As we focus on our heart chakra, feel that joy. We don't have to give it a name. Experience what it is to feel joy inside. Feel it explode as it fills us with tingles of joy throughout our bodies. Feel the joy of how much we are one with the Universe.

Feel how lucky we are to be taught at this moment and the wonder of our lives unfolding as this opportunity is happening. Just to have the intent of understanding is all we need. Let's allow it to fill us.

Now, we're going to bring our hands back down to their normal position. Hopefully, we're not sitting in front of something we could hit; if so, move away. Take a deep breath, bow down to the floor, and think: *with this breath like a wave crashing into the shore, I'm releasing myself to the Universe.*

We breathe out. It's as if we've been entirely exposed to the Universe. When we breathe in, we believe the Universe is filling us; rebuilding us better than we were before. It's going to perfect us to a higher level as we breathe in.

We may say Namaste, which means: I bow to the God within you or the perfection within you.

We bow to God saying, "I acknowledge and respect You as a higher consciousness."

When we're done, simply relax. Let's move our feet out of the position. We're not going to talk if we're with other people; we don't want to be disturbed. This is our *now time.*

Multi-Dimensional Meditation in a few, easy steps:

- *Find a comfortable position sitting half-lotus or in a chair*
- *Focus on your body*
- *Become aware and follow the sensation of your breath coming in and out of your nostrils*
- *Take three deep breaths in and exhale, clearing your mind of thoughts*
- *Place two fingers on your chi chakra, focusing on the touch*
- *Move to your heart chakra, with a great big smile. Radiate joy*
- *Move to your mind chakra*
- *Take a deep breath, and bow down to the floor, releasing yourself to the Universe*
- *Breathe back in and sit up. Sit and enjoy the experience*

After meditation, several things are going to happen. The first few minutes we're going to feel very calm. We want to think about this feeling. You want to think: *how does it feel to be this calm? I haven't felt this calm in a long time.* It's not like a sleeping calm, or a wake up calm. It's similar, but different.

The second thing we're going to do is look around the room. We'll notice after a thirty-minute meditation, everything becomes a little brighter, as if there is a bit more light coming from somewhere. We'll notice everything seems a little clearer, like having a new shirt.

When we look around, everything has new brilliance to it: the chair, couch, carpeting, everything. It's a subtle difference. It's not huge or distinct, but in a way it is.

It's as if some part of us is seeing from a different perspective. We want to enjoy this, especially if we take a walk after we meditate, and look at the trees and grass.

Grass that's been mowed, we tend to look at it with wonderment and smell a bouquet of flowers and scents more pleasant than what we remember. Most people are so asleep they forget to experience life. They're like automated machines. When we come out of a meditative state, we're attuned deeper than before.

If we allow ourselves, we can experience life the way we did when we were children. Every scent has a very peculiar feeling. Every sound ignites a certain joy within our spirit. Everything has the feeling of being new. We've forgotten this as we've grown older. You need to find this again.

What's going to help us find our inner spirit, peace, or growth is in its acknowledgement. It's what we call *awareness*.

One thing quite automated about the human body is our breathing process. We do it almost unconsciously. Breath is critically important for many reasons. Philosophically, breath is the first thing we do when we come into the world. It's the last thing we're going to do when we die.

When we start to get excited or upset, people say, "Breathe into a paper bag. Calm down. Breathe slowly."

There's a truth to this advice. Our psyche, our minds seem to be very connected to our breathing pattern. If we're breathing quickly, we'll find our minds are racing and the Babbler is freer to throw stuff at us.

If we consciously make an effort to slow our breathing, in taking control of it, we'll find our minds become quiet. The Babbler steps away from distracting us, which allows us to have clarity. So, our breathing has a huge effect.

It's one of the things we can take control of, which is normally automated. We don't think about it; we're just breathing. If we get excited we won't pay attention to how fast we're breathing.

If we decide to think about our breathing, choosing to slow it down, the effect will make a huge difference. When we meditate, we think about our breathing; we set a certain pace. By doing this, we're preparing ourselves to go into higher states of mind to allow Prana to move into us.

Prana is God. God is a perfect level of force. God, this energy, loves all life, all things. If we simply ask for It to move towards us, It will. It wants to be our friend. It's like a puppy dog. I hate to put it that way, but have you ever known a happy puppy that doesn't want friends? It wants to be our friend but It needs us to acknowledge It. We need to say, "I know you're there. I see you." God will not impose Its will on us. It doesn't want to bother us. If we open ourselves up to God, and are willing, It's willing to come and fill us. It's willing to allow us to grow the way trees, plants, and lives grow under certain conditions.

Prana needs us to be calm. The Force doesn't want us to feel negativity. We need to stop and clear our minds to remain calm. We need to recognize meditation is a choice; we choose to meditate.

When we do this, we're saying, "I'm prepared for You."

When we have prepared our state of consciousness in such a way we can receive It well, that's when It will come to us.

With different systems, there are different approaches. With Hatha yoga, which is more of a physical or breathing yoga, we focus on energy going down into our bellies then out. We're not focusing on oxygenating our bodies and physically revving it up.

Before we meditate, we can do some deep breathing. We can inhale down into our bellies then release it when we focus on spiritual methods, separating our physical bodies.

We need to designate mental time to nurture our minds, inner well-being, spirit, soul, and consciousness. There's very little time we devote to our minds and inner-spirit.

We go to the gym to work out; we go to our jobs to work our brains. However, our mental state is the most neglected part of our being. This is why we don't experience ethereal wellness; we've forgotten. We need to work on it.

Our culture places such emphasis on physical beauty, having objects, owning property, and acquiring money that we're willing to beat ourselves into the ground to obtain these things. We're willing to learn equations, systematic approaches, and structuralization, but we've forgotten the essence and beauty of who we really are. This is the pain that we often feel.

We have this inner part of our soul crying to come alive. Similar to a plant in a box that wants to grow. Maybe we've put it somewhere in a dark part of the room and have forgotten about it. We haven't given it water or anything.

By some miracle, however, one day we look over and see the box has cracked open. There are two tiny leaves crying, "I'm alive."

Guilt-ridden, we think, *oh, my God. Maybe I should water this thing and place it by the sun.* The point is, there is something inside of us saying we need to be awakened. We need to be acknowledged. We need to have some attention.

Certain spiritual breathing techniques have different purposes. We'll learn spiritual breathing techniques in another session in great magnitude. The technique we're learning now will get us where we need to be. It's what is going to get the job done.

If we follow our breath down, bottom line, it associates us too much with the physical body. When we follow the breath in a rhythmic path by our noses, it gives us a feeling similar to a heartbeat. It puts us into a trance-like state from being in the womb, per se.

Eventually, we're going to forget about our breathing and focus only on touch. We're setting our bodies in a sense of stasis or relaxation. It's like singing a lullaby to put a baby to sleep then tiptoeing out of the room so we can explore or have a moment of peace. It's not that we don't love the baby in the other room; we're simply saying we need to experience something different.

When we're breathing with this system, focusing on the tip of our noses is like singing a lullaby to our physical bodies. In essence, we're saying we won't accept such a demand being placed on us. Our physical bodies are going to distract us, but we're trying to stack up as much as we can in our favor.

By focusing on the chakras, it's like saying we are going to go take a Calgon bath to relax and investigate some other world, or do something for ourselves. This is the difference with this system of meditation. It takes the best systems and integrates them to give us the most powerful experience in the fastest way.

Some people may ask how we know the fastest way is the best way? Why do it this way? Well, every group believed their system of meditation was the best and fastest way at the time. What's the difference if we're using some other system? At the time, it was cutting edge to get us where we could go. In the end, it's results that matter.

Are there experiences I should expect? How long does it take to experience something?

Let me talk about some of the experiences I have had during meditations and what to expect when experiencing this technique. I'll cover a few you will experience, given enough time. If we use this system for thirty minutes a day, twice a day, we will experience great results. If we keep working with it, even within the first few days we can have results. Generally, it takes one to two months. It keeps getting better; it never gets worse. We keep hitting higher plateaus because we're learning to work with our energy - if we can remain consistent.

Every day we will experience something new. Don't worry, we won't get bored. It gets more intense each time, more gratifying. During the first gratifying experience, we'll think to ourselves: *how can it get any better than this?* It does. It's hard to believe, but it will.

Some people say, "I've meditated for a week. My friends who are doing it have seen different things and had different experiences, but I haven't seen anything."

My response, "How have you been?"

They say, "Why, I've been fine."

I ask, "How did you feel before you started doing this? Did you have a reason you chose to try this, or did you do it for the heck of it?"

They say, "I was having problems. I was depressed and not feeling like I was enjoying life. I had some issues and stresses."

I say, "You just said you feel fine now. Do you feel fine?"

They say, "Well, yes, I do."

I ask, "How long have you been feeling fine?"

They say, "Well, probably for the last five days or so."

I ask, "When did you start meditating?"

They say, "Oh, about five days ago."

I say, "Therein lies your answer."

The meditation is working on what we need first. We cannot get to a higher place or find that other door we discussed until our frequency is right. If we have emotional issues that need to be healed, it's going to work on that first. It's going to take the amount of time it needs to fix it, but it will be fixed.

If we don't currently have emotional problems, and are straightened out in every other area, we're going to start having these other experiences more than likely. It's tuning and setting us in a certain way to ready us for what we're going to be. It will never push us into something we're not ready for. It doesn't work that way.

It's putting all our parts together like a car being tuned up. While the car is out of shape, we're not going to be able to do one hundred miles per hour; it's going to putter and jerk around. However, if it gets a tune-up, it will perform at a more optimal level.

When we meditate we're tuning ourselves up, especially under this system. We will be rewarded by our meditation efforts each time with a better experience, until we're ready to perform flawlessly and effortlessly in higher regions because we're meditating at our highest performance level.

We've been working our energy. It gains progressively as we work with it. It rewards us so we can have greater experiences to get to where we're trying to go.

Another thing we'll experience while we're meditating, other than the Babbler, is a feeling we're elongating. We're going to feel like our shoulders and heads are about two to three feet above our hipline, which is on the floor.

What's going on? Our astral bodies are beginning to feel energies; it's stretching, moving, and feels like it's doing certain things. For instance, we'll perceive our bodies are tilting way over to the left. Then we'll open an eye and see we're not. We're sitting upright.

One could say it's a form of the Babbler, but it's also energy stretching and moving. When we first started walking did we get up to hop, skip, and tap dance? No. We had to learn by trial and error; we bumped, tripped, fell, and stubbed our toe. This is how we all learn.

As we build our energy fields, we'll experience other parts of ourselves we haven't even begun to explore or were aware existed. Only on rare occasions have we felt it.

At some point we've all experienced lying down on our bed, relaxing. Suddenly, we jump because we felt a jerk or ourselves falling. That's our astral body moving slightly above us and our brain tells us we can't do that.

When we meditate we're building these energies up. Our energy field is stretching to the left; it's moving to the right. It's like a baby walking; it's learning. That's what's happening. We have to go along with it. What should you be focusing on? The touch.

What matters is to stay focused on the touch. It will straighten itself out. It will right itself when it's ready. Don't worry about it. It's not a concern. Nothing horrible is going to happen. We will always find our way back because we can never truly leave ourselves.

When people perceive they are out of body, they don't understand they're really not completely out of their bodies. If you ask anybody who's experienced it, if they were aware of themselves, they'll say yes. To them, it was comparable to being in two places at the same time.

It's not that we leave our bodies. It's like we stepped out of ourselves and at the same time perceived ourselves.

This perception can be compared to a probe. For example, this planet's a living organism. When a satellite is shot into the air, is it the planet? In a way, yes, because it's made of the planet. What it's doing is observing itself. It's not really the planet; it's a probe of its consciousness able to communicate with itself, sending data back down to its main consciousness.

When we *leave*, our energy body builds up from Prana. It's doing strange things and we don't have full control over everything, yet. We're sending a probe outside our bodies; it's looking at us. We think: *that's me floating above my body.* It's not; it's a probe.

It's a different thing, which will be taught more in-depth when the time comes. It's mind-blowing what we'll be able to do with it.

During meditation we're going to experience some unusual things, but remember fear is not the problem. Being in constant fear is. If we fear everything we're experiencing, we'll stop facing it because it's too overwhelming. It won't hurt us. Everything we experience during meditation is intended to heal us. Sometimes, when we're meditating other things will happen.

Always meditate in a room with light. A well-lit room is good; never meditate in a dark room, which suggests a dark presence. When we open our eyes, we can't see very well. We want to focus on positive, high, good energy; not dark, methodic energy. Candles, although beautiful, are not what we want to rely on for lighting either.

In our meditation, when we shut our eyes, we have light coming from the back. It provides a sense of safety, well-being, and life. Light is represented by lightness, not heaviness. It's represented by this vibration. Anything we can use to catalyst our minds with positivity we want to work with. Therefore, always be in a nicely-lit room.

I remember many years ago, I had my eyes closed and was sitting on the floor with a group. It was a nicely-lit room. I was sitting in the circle meditating, having a wonderful meditation. I was very relaxed and probably feeling proud of myself without thinking about it, just feeling the experience was great. I loved it.

Then suddenly, someone started a strobe light, boom-boom. I thought: *what in hell are these? Somebody in this room is flipping the light switch.* Bewildered, my thoughts continued: *I can't take it anymore. What is going on?* Now, I was babbling. I was losing my concentration.

I opened one eye and it was nothing. The room looked perfectly normal. Everybody was sitting, doing their meditation. Nothing was going on. Again, I thought: *what the heck; what's this all about?*

I closed my eye, thinking: *I'm meditating and feeling good, again. We're cruising and in a good place.*

Suddenly, someone was hitting the light switch again! Or so it seemed. Annoyed, I thought: *I'm going to catch them now.*

I opened my eye; no one was there. Confused, I thought: *there's no way somebody could get to that light switch and sit back down. Why isn't everybody else complaining?*

As we're meditating and drawing in Prana, we're changing our physical fields of energy and it's adjusting us like a tune up. It's energy that dusts us off and gets us to move a little. Let's get this stiff energy inside of us to limber up. Let's do some rock and roll, disco, and a little limbo. Let's liven it up. When it's done, it settles into a flexible, healthier form of consciousness and energy. It is a good thing.

If I had just sat there and let it go, eventually the boom-boom would have faded and gone away. It's a matter of trust. Why did I open my eye? *Fear.* There was no threat; I knew there wasn't any threat.

Who cares if somebody is flipping the switch? What should have I been focusing on? The touch. As we practice, we move into higher stages dealing with different experiences.

It's going to get crazier. As we meditate, we're going to get to a point where we will have such visions we'll swear we are not in the room at all. We'll meditate and the room will cease to exist.

There could be a stereo blaring music and we'll believe it isn't playing anymore. Again, the room has ceased to exist.

We're in this void of absolute peace and calm with clarity in our minds that's so soothing. It's not like we're afraid because it's dark. We're not fearful of anything; it's pure nothingness. It's like before time began, before any universe.

It's just us experiencing the absolute void of nothingness, purity, not even dust. It's okay and feels good. We're going to think: *wait a minute. I don't want to stay here forever. What's going on?* Now, we're babbling. We'll open our eyes and we're back here again.

These are meditation phases we go through. We have to conquer our fear. Once we conquer our fear, we become the master. We somehow blossom from this.

What is dark turns gray. As we accept it and stay focused, it begins to change from gray to light.

As I sat there looking at the gray, I began to see what appeared to be a structure in the distance. I took a breath in and I smelled moisture, like ocean moisture. As I looked,

I began to see the cuttings of beautiful pine trees all around me and fog rolling in between them. I look to the side and I saw an orange, shiny light.

As I continued to look, I saw an ocean and the sun rising. The beams of light were bursting through the pine trees. I'm filled with tranquility and perfection of life. It's so uplifting. I sat there to experience it.

Do we want to stay there? We need to experience it, but not get caught into it. Let it go and see where we're going to go next. Move beyond it.

I've had so many profound experiences early in my youth. I became accustomed to them over time.

One particular case was when I was at the YMCA meditating with some people; working with and teaching them. We had metal chairs on a cement floor. As I was meditating I reached that dark place again. There was nothingness, pure black. All of a sudden, I saw what looked like a silvery spark of light. It reminded me of my grandparents' black and white television. Whenever we turned it on or off, a silver line would appear then pop away.

First, I saw the silver line then I saw it pull across like a string. It looked like a silver light string. I watched it as it began to widen. I floated into absolute nothingness. I thought: *this is great. This is something I've never seen before. This is why I'm meditating; it's something to get out of it.*

It appeared to stretch so wide, I couldn't see the top or bottom. Then I realized it wasn't getting wider; it was already huge. It was so far away and it was moving toward me at the speed of light.

I noticed it was not really light, more like mercury silver. Not shining or illuminating; it was self-contained. I was in awe thinking: *what is this?*

I didn't feel threatened until I realized it was traveling toward me. It was bigger than anything I had ever experienced. Huge! By the time I thought: *what am I going to do?* It hit me, boom! Every single cell of my body skyrocketed in a pitch, like they were struck with a chime.

I was aware of the sound. I was more aware of the vibration moving through me. I was vividly aware of every single cell of my body, right down to my bone marrow. Then I felt each layer of my energy field, being, and consciousness. Something reached out and felt as though my mother, grandfather, everybody I've ever loved in my life, all at one time, held me. It was like I sighed into them. I surrendered into them—and God touched me for a moment. There was the most wonderful, gratifying, tangible feeling in my spirit.

While this happened for what seemed a long time, there was another part of my body that reacted to the first sudden impact. I was moving in time differently. In one way, I experienced all of this slowly; on another physical level that was slow, but grew fast.

I leapt out of the chair because it looked like a Mack truck was about to hit me. I opened my eyes, but the huge impact already happened, as described earlier.

I brought myself into the now; everything was in slow motion. I felt myself moving slowly and the chair moved slowly. Immediately, it went into natural speed then the chair fell to the ground. I jumped up and looked around, breathing heavily and thought: *oh, my God. Whoa, what just happened?* I shocked everybody in the room.

It is a profound place. It was probably the most exciting and encouraging experience at that point in my life. I thought: *I've got to do this again. But am I going to react the same way? Heck no!*

Anybody can achieve these profound things, but it takes dedication; it takes some time. It doesn't take a lot of time. Everybody's idea of time is different. In America, we want everything yesterday. We've got the McDonald's Effect. Give it to me now.

Understand that if somebody is trying to sell something and says just listen to these frequencies and we'll capture this experience, or wear these glasses and strobing lights are the equivalent to that experience, we know it's a bunch of malarkey. These offerings will do a certain thing, but they do not provide what we need. The Universe has given us everything we need to find it.

When people say we can't experience God directly, we just have to have faith, it's nonsense. God gave us a brain. This means God wants us to find It. If we're told we've got to have faith, that we cannot experience God, see God or directly know God other than what we are told God is, who decided this?

I need more than faith; I *have* more than faith. I have experienced, and firmly understand and believe what and who God is. This knowledge has given me enrichment; this is all that really matters.

You can find this knowledge and enrichment, also. This is why you have a brain. So you can figure it out and get there, to that frequency where God resides, to touch It, see It, and know It. That is if you choose to use it.

Chapter 4

ALISONÈ: GOD & THE SIXTH SENSE

PLEASE PAY ATTENTION to what I'm going to say because it's profoundly important, *profoundly*. To know God, is to be able to truly serve God. Do you understand the profundity of what I'm saying? Most people don't have any idea what God is.

The ideas such people have about God are not remotely close to capturing what God is. Therefore, how are they able to truly serve God and not an ideal or illusion of what they think IT is? They may as well be serving a bicycle they found in the street.

One of the most important things for people to be able to say they serve God, they want to serve God, or they want to be a part of God, is to try and find the truest form of God possible. Otherwise, our efforts to serve God are meaningless. We must seriously consider who and what God is.

Most people who say they want to serve God, ironically haven't looked outside of their own circle of what they believe God to be. Whether a person is Christian, Hindu, Buddhist, or Muslim, they should learn as much as they can about differing theologies and schools of thought.

For instance, if a person decides they want to understand what a flower is, it makes sense to study as many flowers as possible. Also, to know who God is, ask: How can I get to know God better? How can I understand what God is?

God is part of a living organism. The universe is a portion of Its body, Its existence. We are a microcosm of the universe. God does not haphazardly come down to our planet and say,

"Eeny, meeny, miny, moe. You have the gift from me and you don't."

God does not choose anything selectively in that manner; No different than how we choose to influence the functioning of our own inner-universe.

God wants life. God propels the proliferation and forward motion of life. IT wants to experience this dimension, world, and reality. It wants to live. In the same way *we* want to live, It wants to live.

In a micro-verse way, a micro reflection of the larger universe, the white cells of our bodies help to preserve the life and wholeness of our entire being. If they did not help us to preserve our whole being (our bodies), all the red cells and organisms of our bodies wouldn't produce any white cells. We would die because of outside viruses entering our inner-universe to destroy the mechanism giving us life.

On a larger level—macro versus micro—certain individuals or beings are in this dimension to serve the earth as a living organism, so the greater can survive or make it forward to whatever its destiny is. If we can understand even that, already we have a better idea how to serve God. Once we have an understanding of what God is, and have a level of truth within ourselves to understand It, we can begin to serve It.

We have to find God by journeying within ourselves. We are energy, a consciousness of energy that must be observed, studied, and contemplated. We must understand our inner-dimensions, inner-vibrations, and inner-consciousness. We can vibrate our consciousness to approach a vibration where God exists.

We consciously reside between our eyes in our heads. This is where our consciousness resides. In all other parts of our bodies we have awareness. God's consciousness is somewhere as well. It is a vibration, a frequency that's constantly present. It constantly says, "I am here."

The problem is nobody understands how to reach and listen to that vibration. We think too much in terms of distance.

In order to get from here to there, we have to travel a certain distance. God is not far away in those terms, yet seekers everywhere are lost in search of It. God is right here. It is not a matter of distance, as much as it is a need to avail ourselves to tune into and hear what IT, God, is saying.

Adam and Eve are said to have been cast out of the Garden of Eden; however, the garden remained. Eden is all around us. It was our *sight* or ability to see this garden that was removed. It was a *sensory* that was removed.

We have five senses: smell, taste, hear, see, and touch. It's what keeps us in tune with this dimension. It's what keeps us at a certain pace to bring in data that's converted into electrical energy for our minds, for our brains. Everything is converted into energy.

The sixth sense is the window to finding God. The sixth sense is still there but we separated ourselves from it. By discovering this inner-sense, inner-energy, inner-ability we nurture a sensory that has the ability to move us into higher dimensions of energy, higher frequencies. It is only through developing this sense when we may connect with what we are seeking.

In other words, to determine if something is hot or cold, we can reach out and touch it with our hands. Our eyes aren't necessarily going to tell us if something is cold or hot. They'll identify telltale signs such as steam or ice, but our eyes can't tell us definitively; neither can our ears.

If we were deaf, we couldn't hear if someone was yelling around the corner for us. Our sensory is designed to give us knowledge in certain areas where others cannot. It's like dimensions; it's like hidden things. Each sensory has its array of experiences it can offer, answers we are looking for, for our search, our need to expound upon for the one thing that it gives us: *knowledge.* This knowledge is designed to set us free.

This sixth sense has brought us into a region where we should've had this other sense. This ability was lost through the evolution of man. As we developed larger craniums, weapons, and tools, we stopped using regions of our brains.

Humankind would've been more spiritual and in tune with God as a species. We lost this potential, somehow. All of humankind has been trying to find it again. This is the need of all human beings—to establish a relationship with God. Even red cells are trying to find something; they feel they are supposed to do so. Some of us feel it greater than others. What split humankind from this union—evolution. Again, it was the lack of using a certain portion of our brains; however, other senses remained.

The need to find the elusive sixth sense is a natural instinct. The sixth sense is as capable of multiple functions as our hands, eyes, or ears.

Are our ears exclusively designed to hear conversation or can they hear music that moves our spirit? Can our ears hear to let us know of approaching danger, or communication of a different form?

Are our eyes purely designed to see or can they not move our spirit? Can our eyes not save us from approaching danger? Can our eyes not read or tell us about things in general? Can they not deliver knowledge in others ways through the reading of books?

Our tongue, hands, ears, eyes, and nose, all of these sensory don't just serve one specific purpose.

The sixth sense is multi-talented and multi-capable. It has a variety of things it can deliver. It's up to us to discover, engage, and exercise it. So, when we meditate or do spiritual work, what we're really doing is trying to develop that sixth sense, which has been ignored, not been dealt with, and not been trained or developed.

It's very weak initially because it hasn't been exercised like other senses. Other senses have been trained to help us survive; they have been somewhat mandatory in many ways. The ones not necessarily engaged to deal with direct survival are weaker.

For instance, the sense of and ability to smell. The sixth sense is a matter of bringing it forward: the more we use it, the more we become aware of another world.

If we're a musician and listen to music all the time, and we play music, what is it that most of the time we relate to? Music! We hear it all the time, even in doors shutting and people hollering. We hear rhythms and patterns; it's where we exist.

Artists use their eyes. The artist sees all the colors, shapes, and shadows. What happens when we start to use our sixth sense? Our dimensional world comes forward; we begin to see more of reality than others. We see more spirits, entities, dimensional things, and energy.

We experience things on a paranormal level. We reach hyper-dimensional levels of consciousness that other people can't even begin to understand.

The idea is to find ways to get our sixth sense to work, to kick it into gear. Then realize we can do these things at will and experiment to relate to things; we expand on these things.

For people who don't work their sixth sense, of course, it doesn't exist for them. If we never heard anything or weren't able to touch or smell, it would be very hard to relate to, or understand.

The sixth sense is one of the final senses used to connect with God, to find what we're really looking for. It cannot be found solely using our five senses.

We must be complete. Each sense is a tool to find our way back to God. Since we're missing one, it's the loop that all philosophies and teachings are missing. It is the reason why students do not reach enlightenment from other spiritual teachers because they are missing the understanding to meditate to reach higher states of consciousness. We must link the sixth sense. We must exercise psychic abilities.

Those abilities have always been misunderstood, even persecuted as possibly witchcraft. If someone believes another can read their mind, or has powers they do not, they will feel threatened. People would have been so fearful, they push away the development of these abilities and what they really are.

Mystical teachers and schools who once understood these abilities, pushed the knowledge underneath the carpet so they could get along with the red cell world. Humankind was a necessity to build a relationship, so both could successfully achieve their goals.

This is why history has extracted it from books. It's been written certain ways, and openly spiritual people would have to say: *we don't really profess this*. However, in secret teachings, of course they would tell the inner-circle what the deal was.

There is a sixth sense; this is what we need to achieve. We need to develop if we're going to understand or find our connection to God. Don't be afraid of it.

Even now you understand a lot more than the average person does. You're ready for the real thing, aren't you? I'm going to help you find what you're seeking.

We're going to teach students to see, hear, taste, smell, and feel in another unimaginable way. Without this sensory, every spiritual master knows they would never have a successful student.

In order to know God, to truly know God, we need all of our senses. To understand what God is, can't be fully internalized through mere words. I can't wave my hands around and paint a picture that will allow you to realize what God is. All senses are a reflection of God. When we smell something beautiful, it's a piece of God.

Our five senses, no matter how well-tuned, will never definitively capture what we're yearning for—ache, need, or feel—within our spirit. There's something missing.

This is why people go their whole lives, never quite there, never quite complete. We read it in works of poetry. We see it in the works of master artists. We hear it in the greatest musical pieces developed and created.

However, there's something they're still aching for, as if they've made it to the very fringe of what they were really seeking, which is God. It's as if something didn't quite take them there; it's about the sixth sense.

If one learns to meditate and is told not to develop psychic abilities, yet through meditating suddenly we will find enlightenment; this is not correct. It won't happen. The point is, every great spiritual master has demonstrated what would be considered paranormal abilities.

They see into the future, heal the sick. They move objects through their minds. They seemingly have numerous psychic abilities they exhibit in different ways.

They discovered a hyper-dimensional consciousness, which led to their enlightenment. They entered a realm of understanding then cautiously disclosed it because society would find it difficult to accept them. People would've been fearful, causing them to attack or distance themselves. Their reaction would have been reminiscent of the Salem witch trials, just a different century and culture.

There was a political environment, which dictated such things had to be swept underneath the carpet. Consider this, all these people who are meditating, searching to find some form of enlightenment, the vast numbers never make this discovery.

The ones who actually do find it, don't acknowledge it, but have developed the sixth sense within them. They've either incidentally or intentionally looped into its energy. In any event, they found the sixth sense and integrated it with their teaching, the final piece needed to find the higher consciousness.

In order to serve God, we must truly be able to find and understand God. Through the development of our senses, training, pushing buttons, moving emotions to think, and pushing through our minds, hopefully the sixth sense will come forward without us realizing we've entered this level.

In so doing, we start to awaken. We develop our ability to perceive the final puzzle pieces needed to find God. That which we are seeking most in our lives—what is missing inside of us— we ache to understand. More importantly, to understand what it is the Force, God, is asking us to do.

If we don't have ears, how can we hear somebody telling us their need? If we don't have eyes, how are we going to be shown what we need to do? Somebody may write it down for us if we were deaf, particularly in Braille if we were blind.

Imagine the chances of obtaining this information. What are the chances of finding what we're seeking? What if we had to find it without anyone's assistance?

Maybe we need help. A teacher, friend, or someone who's willing to show us what we need to do, how to get there, or how they can extend help to us. In the end, we're talking about obtaining the ultimate piece of information, which may or may not be so readily accessible. This entirely depends upon our level of intensity to understand God. Therefore, we have to respect and realize it's going take a great deal of effort to find what we're seeking.

God is not a man or woman, and we're all past that. God is a living consciousness, an energy. It's an energy that is constantly here, now, in this room, at this very moment. Only our senses don't see it. Similar to the exercise in *The Handbook of the Navigator*, counting the number of F's is seemingly elusive.

If we were deaf right now, we could have blaring music on and everything would seem calm and surreal (ignoring the vibration any bass might make). We would have no idea why the cats abandoned us, or why the neighbors trying to sleep are angry. It would be as serene and beautiful as ignorance can be blissful.

God is here right now. God is absolutely vibrantly loud and full of life. The problem is we cannot experience It fully because we're missing one of the connectors to help us find what we are seeking.

To know our purpose, what it is we are designed to do, and how we are suppose to serve, we need to be in the presence of God. To experience that, what we seek most, lies in our determination to develop this last sensory.

In so doing, we find answers. Through our journey to levels of enlightenment and consciousness, we perceive, understand, and gather pieces to the very puzzle we're supposed to bring together.

Does God love us?

Let me ask a question. How well do you know your body?

A little bit.

A little bit? Do you have a personal relationship with your kidney, liver, and heart? How about your thigh muscle?

No, I don't think so.

If I tried to harm it, what would you do?

Protect it.

Why?

Because it's valuable.

How is it valuable? Would you let me cut your shirt, before I cut your skin?

Yes, of course!

So, you have a sense of devotion to your body, correct?

Yes.

Yet, we know your body is not you. We know it is made of living organisms independently separate from you. You're a coexisting energy being that's somehow hot-wired in with it all. These organisms live to serve you, don't they? Because in serving you, they serve the whole, and the whole allows them to exist. So, it's a three-ring circus, right?

Well, God very much is the same way. God will defend us because It loves us. Yet, we live and die. We have cells every single moment, even as we sit, dying. We have illnesses and poisons going through our bodies. There are numerous amounts of battles we have no idea about.

Sometimes, we come very close to the brink of death, with colds, flus, or diseases. Yet, there is a constant struggle to survive. Are we not using our will to encourage our bodies to live? Bottom line, is there not a part of us that connects with our inner-universe and wants it to fight viruses, wants to survive what it's going through?

Yes, when I get sick I want to get better.
I encourage my body to feel better.

God doesn't necessarily know who and what everybody is. It is not important to know that. It's no more important to God than it is to you and your body. Now, that may sound horrible, like God doesn't really care. God cares; it's a much bigger, expansive thing than we can imagine. We love every part of our bodies and want the best for our bodies. Sometimes we make good decisions; sometimes we make bad decisions.

The reality of it is, when it really comes down to it, we would fight to live and for our bodies to survive. We may not give its survival much thought, but it does not change our devotion to it.

God loves everything. However, it's a different kind of love than we want to perceive. We want to perceive a loving, nurturing relationship like a mother and child. The bond of life is much stronger. It's stronger than even a mother's love for her child.

Are we aware of every single cell in our bodies? Are we aware of any of them? No. We are generally aware of our primary sensory areas.

There are certain areas that are more important to us. Would we knowingly drink poison? Now, somebody may make small arguments about coffee or alcohol, but we're really looking at extreme levels.

The point is, God loves us as individuals as much as we love our individual cells. Yes, God loves us. It doesn't mean that God is specifically aware of each of us. We want to feel like the individuals we are, yet want to know God has specifically identified us, singled us out, and we have a special role. Every living being has a special role to God, whether they're red cells, white cells, planets, or galaxies. Everything's vitally important.

Why should we be angry or disappointed that God doesn't acknowledge us in the way that we want? Who do we think we are, that we are supposed to be selectively chosen and known by God? I propose something different. God gave each of us a brain and intelligence to reach for a higher level. If we want to find God, we have everything we need to do that. Conversely, if we don't want to try, God has given us free will to live our lives the way we want. Isn't that better anyway? We have the power, and we get to choose, to find God or not.

We have to put forth the effort and have the will to find God. If we choose to be in the place to experience God then we must work towards it. Whether it means meditating, developing the sixth sensory, whatever we need to do, we're moving towards God.

It's not like we're walking to God, but in a way we're traveling towards God. We're changing our octaves, vibrations, and tonals, so eventually we're there in that presence. It's about stepping forward.

White cells do it everyday; they have much greater activity in the body than red cells. Red cells do their job in our bodies. White cells feel a need to preserve something greater, whereas the red cell doesn't. The white cells identify the bad guys (viruses), when the red cells couldn't tell the difference.

Why does a white cell acknowledge these things? It's on a higher level of understanding than red cells. Both are critically important, but to the white cell it's not a matter of importance. It's simply a matter of it serving what it needs to do: something greater than itself. It doesn't have to perceive who we are or even know who we are. It knows our presence.

When people get sick, cancer studies and various research indicate when these people are more positive, their immune system increases. White cells get stronger. It's as if some power of the Force is feeding, supporting, and empowering them to fight some kind of disease that's destroying everything.

They're receptive to it because they understand the Force; they know who we are. They may not know each of us individually, just what's in our bodies. They feel and are loyal to us. They're willing to help and fight to the end.

So, white cell relationship with us is greater than red cell relationship because they seek it out. They live at a different level of relationship in our energy field, which is nothing compared to our existence. We're infinitely, ancient compared to them. In retrospect, we want to develop a relationship with this energy field. The more we relate to this energy field the more we're going to understand, perceive, conceive and relate to whatever it is we feel we need to be part of.

It's what's going to complete us. More than likely, we're never going to understand what God is completely; no more than the white cells in our bodies will ever completely understand who we are. This reality is beyond them.

Is it important to understand It? Is it not more important to have our own experience of God no matter how extensive? It'll be extensive enough.

It's about us being able to move into God's presence; being able to understand, communicate, or experience this presence better so we can serve; no more, no less than the white cells in our bodies serve.

We are already within God. God is here. All we have to do is choose to see, to experience. It's a matter of awakening. Every culture, every belief already knows this. The problem is the words fall on deaf ears.

If we are told in Luke, *"Ask, and it shall be given you; seek, and ye shall find; knock, and it shall be opened unto you,"* what is it telling us? It's saying our answer is already here; it's simply a matter of choosing to put forth the effort to reach for it. However, nobody really wants to do so.

They would rather do the red cell thing, automate, and get through life. That's that. In order to find something beyond this, we have to put forth some kind of will, effort, desire to be on another level; a willingness to work for it, then achieve it, be there, and remain there.

Whether it be right and left hemispheres of the brain, or masculine or feminine polarities, to various techniques and training, it makes us stronger, more emotionally stable, and equipped with everything we need to achieve what we're seeking to do.

It helps us become a more complete person in a lot of ways. This completeness is the foundation to each of us being able to move into the sixth sensory, into something higher, without having the demands of smaller problems in our lives constantly distracting us to achieve something that may be very challenging to do.

How can we learn to experience the sixth sense?

We learn by meditating and watching our teacher. We learn by different things, such as how to shift our consciousness.

There are some things that cannot be explained using typical language. I always come up with my own formulas to express or explain it through analogies or makeshift ideas of how to express it. We will learn to breathe, hear, and see in ways we've never done before and sometimes we have.

Sometimes people cross over; it's like ancient memory. They feel a certain way for a moment, or they daze off into this place that feels really good, but it's not about the place at all.

Sometimes, they smell something that triggers a flashback in their minds to intense memories. Other times, they can hear a sound in the distance that moves their spirit. They cross and experience it, but not long enough because they don't know how to hang onto it, or what to do with it when they find it, when they experience it.

Mostly, it's about having some kind of understanding of what all these things are. It's about having some kind of tool to conceive or organize it in such a way we can make it useful to us.

Putting it into perspective, so we can better use it.

In this reality, in this dimension, human beings have to tag and categorize everything in their minds. When we are connected to somebody who understands how the human mind thinks, operates, intellectually perceives, and understands things, it's easier to find a formula to help us get out of this dimension.

We've got to work with what we have, and can't ignore it. If we've got arms and legs, and think a certain way, we've got to work with what we have. It doesn't mean we can't find a way out of it. We have to see how creative we are to do it.

This is where it begins and it's going to initially take time, effort, and knowledge. Philosophical ideas must be understood. We must understand things we're talking about now to understand why we're doing and talking about these things. Why these topics?

We must have an understanding of theoretical formulas. Once we have a good grasp of what the universe looks like theoretically, in terms of how it functions and how God is an organism, it's like some part of our sixth sense starts kicking in.

Look at Helen Keller, a girl who was deaf and blind; she had no real connection with the outside world. She had no perception of our reality because she was missing two of the biggest senses to help put it all together.

As she learned or was forced to learn, more or less, she began to accept the concept of water. It was given a name, and certain textures were given a name. As she became more educated, her world exploded. Although she lacked certain sensory, she entered our world when she compensated for it in other ways.

She was always on the outer edge, always wanting to know, but never really able to enter, share relationships, communicate, and to experience. I watched a documentary during which she said before she actually understood everything, she had an understanding of what certain things were, but it was always out of her reach. She didn't have a word or understanding for it, so she could never experience it; she was denied.

As you learn how to understand dimensions, feelings, vibrations, and tonals, I'm going to show you that you experience it everyday. You just have no idea you're doing it. You are always on the edge, but never able to really enter.

The point is all of a sudden we just awaken and begin to understand; it just makes sense, the same way Helen Keller experienced her mental breakthrough. When she was being taught, she didn't get it. Every time her hands were put in water, her teacher, Ann Sullivan, would spell out water in her hands, so she could feel what it was, but she didn't get it.

Then suddenly, one day, she got it. It was like a light bulb turning on in her head. Now, this reality penetrated her very being, so she could begin to experience it.

In order to understand hyper-dimensional consciousness, understand God, and all of these other things being referenced, it's going to take time. As we are being shown different things, given examples to understand things, or shown how to do certain things, it's building an awakening. It's building something until all of a sudden, we simply understand.

Then we'll say, "I get it."

The response will be, "Okay, now I'm going to take you even higher."

We may ask ourselves, "Why wouldn't I understand this right away?"

It's like an entirely new level of sensory. We need our first level of sensory to begin to understand the next level.

If we've never used our hands to touch something, it would be a major breakthrough. It would be another breakthrough to learn how to make pottery without it collapsing or warping. It is another thing to learn how to play an instrument and experience emotions at another level.

Doorways are opened by using our hands. Doorways are opened through our eyes. We may perceive beauty in a flower, but it's another thing to perceive beauty in artwork. To watch people gyrating their bodies through dance and understand it, is to perceive beauty at another level. As we experience breakthroughs in our consciousness, the idea is to keep learning.

This is what makes us angelic in the end and refines us into enlightenment. That's what makes us compassionate, beautiful, and understanding. Once we have a greater palate of understanding, we realize how trite things like ego and things related to it really were when we had a limited understanding of them.

We can't be expected to understand more until we are enlightened. The most we can hope for is to have the patience and compassion for ourselves to get there through work, effort, and learning.

Many people cut themselves short thinking, falsely, they've got it all. Limited by their own ego, and also by their lack of vision for how vast the Universe really is. They get to a pivotal point and believe that's it. They are seeing universes; their whole body is humming and vibrating this love of God. They don't believe it can be greater than that. Even at that level they become self-consumed.

It is almost impossible for them to conceive it can go to another, higher level.

Awakening is a process, not a point. Enlightenment, which they truly never reached, is not a destination. You don't become enlightened and that's it, you're done. It goes on.

It will never end. The day it ends, is the day we peacefully leave the universe. True death, as death in this life is not really an end; it depends on what you choose.

Even the universe, God, is still growing and evolving. It is changing. How can you expect to suddenly figure out the universe? As good as it gets, it always gets better. That's wonderful; the amazing process of creation. Who would want it to stop? Who wants it to be completed at some point?

We should always strive to experience God, and be thankful for what we can comprehend. Never seek to put it in a box. It always goes on.

What really defines consciousness as man separates?

Consciousness is multi-faceted. There's not one specific definition. For the most part, consciousness is an echo of life; it is some level of self-awareness. However, even in self-awareness we tend to remain relatively asleep. Is this considered conscious or unconscious?

In life, we react to things, which biochemically is just an equation. Not consciousness. For instance, are computers conscious? Can they not multi-task? Do they not respond to certain commands? When do we realize whether they are conscious or not conscious? The point is, if we put a super chip in a computer, to give it a thousand variables to a thousand reactions, and it seamlessly reacts to everything appropriately as we see it, does it mean it's conscious now?

Human beings are unconscious in many ways but we think we're conscious. We're programmed to respond in specific ways through our emotions, feelings and how we react.

People are very automated yet some spark of consciousness can still exist. It is not a black-and-white condition. There's a lot of amazing beauty in things. Sometimes I'm surprised by something.

I contemplate, "That's a little piece of consciousness; now, that's reality."

Genuine spiritual contemplation leads to true consciousness in the end. We almost have to remove ourselves from everything; isn't this what meditation is about?

We can remove ourselves from things in life that contribute to random thinking, or what appears to be random thinking. It's not; we simply react to things, so we are kept in a program. Something happens, we respond. All of these things are a program initiating all of our responses. It's very complex.

When we meditate and extract ourselves from all thought, we only have one goal and that is to possibly head into some arena of true consciousness. Once we cease all the other programming then we enter this inner-place, a more unique place.

There is no script there for us. It's something beyond; it's a different consciousness. Can we experience true consciousness or do we create true consciousness? Both, but it's hard and part of what some people would call enlightenment.

Everybody has a level of consciousness. Everybody has the potential of discovering true consciousness. In some ways, we all have a portion of it to react to things, but there's a greater portion that controls our consciousness.

We have to acknowledge with the bit of consciousness we have, and empower it to awaken. We have to awaken to the greatest level of consciousness we can and exercise it more. It's a pretty tough thing to tackle.

In some ways red cells are not as fully conscious as white cells, which seem to somehow have a higher level of consciousness. The more consciousness they begin to understand, achieve, or maintain determines the level of ability or spiritualness to perceive what's really going on around them.

We can sit here all day long and talk about what God is, but it doesn't really mean any more than what everybody else is claiming. The real answer is to show you so you can show yourself. I can lead you to water. I can't make you drink it, but I can help you find it.

Most spiritual people whether they be Christian, or whatever, claim the same thing. They give a formula to find God; we all have our ideas about what we think this formula is, which is a matter of perception.

When we meditate, we can be in such a spiritual place of calmness; in some way God is present with us. We can feel it if we choose to do so. We can have God come into us if we allow it. If we want to experience God, we just have to surrender everything we think we are and remove ourselves from everything holding us in this reality. We must set ourselves free.

If we are set free, there's nowhere else to go because God is always there. We simply realize what's been there the whole time. When we allow ourselves to go to such a place, we experience and receive God.

When I have done spiritual things, when I have shown miraculous things, never once has it been when I've been in the DOE. Never once has it been when I've been Eric. It's happened when I surrender everything in my heart.

When we let God step into us, it's surrendering. God orchestrates everything and we're where It needs us to be. It's energy, so It needs to use someone in this dimension and we're a receptive tool for God to use. This is really what it's about. It's about allowing ourselves to humbly be a representation for God to step through.

It's a beautiful thing, like a hum, a song; like being hugged by someone who loves you, a mother or grandmother. It's feeling the strength of an army, without being about power. It goes beyond words.

It's profound. Coming from being in a clear, receptive state of mind. We must allow It to step through us. God won't approach us to dwell within us if we're unwilling. We have to understand our energy and have such a relationship with our consciousness we can allow It to flow through us. This is really the key and it comes from practice.

This receptivity comes from being in tune and understanding. We have to be careful we don't freeze up and don't panic. We have to understand what it is as well as the situation. God is so conscious of us, not wanting to hurt us, It will not approach us if there is a chance we will be startled.

This is how responsive and kind God is. It's so respective of us as a force, as a power. It wants us to really be willing to openly work with It to work through us. Of course, understanding this balance connects with everything discussed thus far. Any questions?

How does God compare to the intelligence and consciousness of evil?

God is profoundly beyond evil. There's no comparison if we look at the whole. We've got to understand: God is multidimensional. When I say God is the body of the universe, it refers to this dimension. Meaning, God is presently here; it's what frequency we're on, but more importantly, God is also in other dimensions, in other universes, or whatever we want to call it. God resides in all those places. Dimensions can move up in higher octaves, and in the highest octaves only God exists. There is no evil there; there is no counter force of energy.

Now as God moves down in these octaves of energy, which each is a slice, a dimension of space, which is our universe, per se. There could be another universe, but as we move up in these octaves, they're higher and begin to change. They become higher energy universes, frequencies, etcetera.

Even this is an energy universe. Nothing is really what we think it is. God approached this dimension with Its energy, and created what has been attributed to the Big Bang. As we keep changing octaves of energy, we have different laws of physics and reactions to God's action. In this dimension, the creation of the universe resulted in a counter-force, which is the Darkside; what most would consider evil.

The Darkside, in this particular case, is anti-life, meaning anti-matter. We're all matter. Our physicality is matter and because the Darkside doesn't want us, it wants to remove the presence of matter.

Now, the highest level of matter between energy and physicality is consciousness. Everything we touch, feel, everything is matter, but it's converted into a higher format of matter due to energy, our consciousness.

So, the Darkside sees life on planets as a threat because planets on a larger scale are more the meat to the Darkside rather than dealing with the microbes. We're microbes. It deals with the microbes because the microbes can destroy the whole of the larger.

It's the same thing, micro/macro, our own bodies. We're not destroyed by a giant virus coming over, knocking us over the head and killing us. On a micro-level it tries to destroy us from a lower level on out.

It's the same as living beings. There are people, who have very dark abilities—the Darkside; or people who practice the dark arts; or call it what you want. It's a whole conversation in itself, but they tap into this counter force, this dark side energy. They use it for their own good, but it's like a virus in their bodies.

In the same way, a virus can operate and mimic other things in our bodies, causing white cells to figure it out and hopefully defeat it. In essence, if we're asking: how intelligent is the Darkside? It's extremely intelligent, but not as intelligent as God.

This does not mean it's not a threat. The Darkside is a powerful threat in this dimension. In some ways, it mimics God, but has completely opposite intensions or desires.

God is certainly keeping a step ahead of the game. However, by the same token, the Darkside has won many battles. How much will God walk away with in the end? This is the real debate of the internal battle constantly between the two in this dimension.

Does God allow the Darkside, or evil forces, to exist in infinite dimensions?

God doesn't let the Darkside exist in other dimensions because it just can't exist there, but that's an entirely different topic. The point is, God allows the Darkside to exist. It's a challenge that makes God think. Of course, if God steps out of place once, It will be gobbled up. The Darkside won't offer a hand to help God up. There is a risk in God exploring this way but God is curious. Humans reflect how God is because we're a part of It.

Do we flirt with disaster when we're curious? Why would we ride a motorcycle knowing we're flirting with disaster on a higher level? Why do we fly in airplanes? Why do we scuba dive? Why do we feed sharks or lions with meat?

In a sense, we are a small reflection. God looks at the Darkside, wanting to counter it, but acknowledges there's so much in this dimension, in life, to experience. It's not just flirting with disaster for the sake of it. It's holding off disaster to experience everything else that's wonderful.

As we're riding a motorcycle, we feel the sun on our face, the wind in our hair, and the open freedom. We're aware of the risk and we try to be careful.

This what God's doing in this universe. It is experiencing the immense, profound amount of possibilities. By the same token, It has to be extremely careful because there's always something attempting to counter Its efforts.

We're constantly breathing in viruses designed to kill us. There's constantly an array of preventive battles going on to ensure we make it as long as we can, the best we can. Since there's a counter force, does it mean we shouldn't exist? We should just pack it up? Or do we live life as much as possible? The goal is to try to live life as much as we can.

When you say God is trying to experience the universe, isn't God all-knowing?

Who said God is all knowing?

That's what I thought because it's God.

God is not all knowing. God is all knowing to man, because man is very limited in his intelligence. But does that mean that we have to perceive that in comparison to us that God is all knowing? Or is it wrong to assume that God isn't all knowing and because we can't say for sure that's the case? If God was all knowing, I give you this one argument. Then what is the need for any of this? What difference would it make? Why would you play the same video game if you knew every single thing that it was going to do before it did it? Well, in reality if you knew everything it was going to do before it did it, you wouldn't even bother to do it because you've already done it all. It has already happened.

The universe is a curiosity for God. Its coming into this dimension is to see what is going to happen. What are all the possibilities? It's to experience this immense complex experience, but there are things even God doesn't know. And thank God; I'm sure It's thoroughly entertained. The point is curiosity. God is a young God in my opinion. It could be 20 ka-trillion years old. What is that compared to time itself? Does time even exist? So God is experiencing just like we do on a micro level. What would you do if there was nothing for you to do all day? Tell me. If you knew everything, what would you do? There's one thing you would do. You would try to find the one thing you don't know. I think it's a very simple equation. Does that disappoint you?

No.

God wants to live. God wants to experience. God wants to understand. It's just on a much bigger level than what we are. It's just on a whole different level, a whole different extreme.

A Christian often boxes God in with their ideals, to make God what they want It to be, rather than let it be what it is. It is hard to let go of that. I feel like I need God to love and acknowledge me, even though I see the truth of what you are saying.

The point is, God does love and acknowledge us. It may not look the way we expect it to look. It's the vanity and ego people talk about all the time. It is a form of vanity and ego to think God should love us on our terms.

Are there finite dimensions?

Well, what is your interpretation of finite dimensions?

Is God at the top? Then going down, is there a lower frequency where God does not exist?

There are many, but we need to be careful when we use the term frequency because frequency is a relatable human term in proportion to sound. This is how the brain catalogs ideas. Frequencies are referenced as an analogy to help describe something to people who may not understand, which may cause confusion by using the term dimension, or multiple dimensions.

For the sake of argument, does God reside in one dimension? No, God is multi-dimensional. In how many dimensions can God exist? It's infinitive, why bother counting? Do you think there's a highest and a lowest? In terms of human beings, we are forced to think in terms of higher and lower.

There are regions God purely exists in, and can only exist in. Additionally, there are places where darkness exists. It does not exist, however, until God enters because there must be a reaction.

It begs the question: are there places where the Darkside purely exists? No, because if it purely existed then there is no existence of matter; there's nothing. It does not matter. What matters is there's a reaction here and the Darkside wants to remove it. It's a countering reaction.

Some say we need darkness. It can only exist if there's light, and light can only exist if there's darkness. Evil can only exist if there's good. Well, there's probably some truth to this, but that can also lead to action and non-action, or reality becoming functional or non-functional which is a whole other debate. Keep in mind, I already said there are places where only God exists, without Darkside but not the other way around. What is important to us, as material beings? What matters is somewhere there is a middle ground. It doesn't necessarily mean it's specifically the middle ground for our dimension, but it's an arena in itself.

In a few ka-trillion eons of time, God will walk away from dealing with this because it won't matter. It will move on to other things and evolve beyond this. Right now, for us to think in terms of ka-trillions of years is such an enormous expanse of time, we might as well call it infinite. What's more important is working on what God wants now because that's what we're here to do. This is the goal. Whether we can achieve it or not will be determined by the things we're involved in, here and now.

Is there reincarnation?

Absolutely, there's reincarnation. The majority of people, red cells, do not have reincarnation. White cells, however, have reincarnation. It's a necessity to carry over information. Like white cells in our bodies. We never catch the same cold twice because our white cells remember how to defeat it, or what the sequence or frequency is to defeat the viruses it dealt with previously.

It's a micro-soul, or a conscious throw over of data. On a planet level, there are human, or white cell, memories that carry over knowledge that goes from one life to another.

Is free-will absolute?

What do you mean; is free will absolute?

Does the soul have absolute or not so much control, but choice in the course of its life?

A soul has more choice as it progresses, as we become more powerful and build our souls.

A soul can have other bodies inside of itself just like we would say these are our main bodies; the flesh and brain, the mind and energy body. We have multiple bodies. As we develop multiple bodies, we become stronger. In doing so, we have more options in this dimension, this universe, to move beyond ourselves.

That is the ultimate journey, the ultimate devotion. It is true evolution; a development beyond not only the brain, but the discovery of our multi-dimensional being; our multi-dimensional consciousness. It is awakening.

The Next Step is Yours

Higher Balance Institute is dedicated to giving you the tools and knowledge needed to empower yourself and transform your life. The purpose and mission of the Institute is to awaken the world one mind at a time. Toward fulfilling this goal, we know the greatest results come when you can experience something for yourself rather than solely reading about it.

Guided Meditation

Readers of this book receive special reader-only material that expands on the knowledge you have gained here. Included is a free guided meditation to lead you through the Multi-Dimensional Meditation technique.

To receive your additional material, visit
www.meditationwithineternity.com
then select the Readers-Only option.

What are you waiting for?

If you would like to continue your Higher Balance experience, we suggest reading *Bending God: A Memoir* by author, Eric Robison. It details real-life, reality-altering experiences using this knowledge. Visit www.bendinggod.com.

Beyond This Book

To discover techniques and knowledge to experience awakening yourself beyond what has been discussed in this book, please visit us at: www.higherbalance.com.

Higher Balance Institute's programs were created with the purpose of stimulating and activating the dormant sixth sense, the missing link to spiritual awakening.

Higher Balance programs are provided as books, at-home audio courses, or a self-paced online system that comes with everything you need to accomplish your goals. It is the most unique and powerful program of its kind in the world. Join us and the thousands of others worldwide who have been transformed through the Higher Balance experience.

Higher Balance Institute
515 NW Saltzman Road #726
Portland, Oregon 97229
Web: www.higherbalance.com

Sit vis vobiscum.

CPSIA information can be obtained at www.ICGtesting.com
Printed in the USA
LVOW121353260113

317377LV00004B/7/P